MAJESTIC DESTINY

KINGDOM HOPE IS RISING

CURTIS H. TUCKER

Last Chapter
Publishing

MAJESTIC DESTINY
published by Last Chapter Publishing LLC.
PO Box 2385, Redmond, OR 97756
www.lastchapterpublishing.com

©2011 by Curtis H.Tucker

International Standard Book Number
978-0-9816514-6-0
1. Christian living. 2. Eschatology. 3. Christian theology.

Scripture quotations are from the *New American Standard
Bible* (NASB) 1960, 1977, 1995 by the Lockman Foundation
unless otherwise specified.

Cover design
Chris Gilbert
Gearbox Studios

Ordering information:
www.majesticdestinybook.com
or to order bulk quantities call
541.280.3152

ENDORSEMENTS

If you are looking for an outstanding example of 'rightly dividing the Word of Truth" in an area of massive misunderstanding in the church today, then this book is for you! You will be changed forever when you grasp the difference between the Kingdom and Heaven as well as eternal life received as a gift and rewards earned by your good works. I heartily recommend this book.
Bruce Wilkinson, Author Prayer of Jabez *and* You Were Born for This

As someone who has been writing for years on the need to distinguish between the gift of eternal life and the prize of eternal rewards, I found this biblically accurate, Christ-centered message immensely refreshing. I'm excited to have a book I can give to believers that will encourage them to live for Jesus and the world to come.
Ed Underwood, Pastor, Church of the Open Door and Author, Reborn to be Wild

Over a period of many years I have read nearly every book on the subject of the kingdom of God, but this one stands apart because it gripped and excited me like none other I have read. I must also admit that I have never read anything on the subject with such consistent development and interpretation. Let me say it again, no other book on this topic has kept me interested and excited me in the way that this one does. Without any hesitation whatsoever I recommend this book as a must read for all. It will grip you and motivate you to live from a place of assurance and security in God's love for His glory.
Dr. Earl Radmacher, Th.D., President Emeritus, Western Seminary (Portland, Oregon)

Writing with a theologian's mind for harmony, an exegete's eye for context, and a pastor's heart for people, Curtis Tucker has drawn us back to the text of the written Word and to the heart of the Living Word. This little book may well rock your world...in a good way, of course!
Stu Weber, Author Tender Warrior *and* Infinite Impact

Curtis has given us a magnificent vision of the final destiny of man. In a well written and very inspirational manner he clearly articulates the important distinction between the free gift of salvation and the prize we can have, reigning with him, in the future Kingdom. Here is a book you can pass out with confidence to encourage the weary, and challenge the lukewarm. Well done!
Joseph C. Dillow, TH.D., Author Reign of the Servant Kings
Founder Biblical Education by Extension International (BEE).

ACKNOWLEDGMENTS

This project has been in the works for many years in my mind and study. The message itself is not novel or original; it has been in the ancient text all along, so many thanks to God for revealing it in His Word, and for the empowerment to write it in the pages herein. And thanks also to Jesus for His gratis offer of salvation, which I took by faith when I was nineteen. I only regret wasting so much time in resistance before then.

Thanks to the wonderful and supportive congregation of Redmond Community Church, and to the dedicated staff and elders whom I have the privilege of serving alongside. Special thanks to Steve Rodine, my friend and comrade in the ministry for many years, for doing all the stuff I am no good at, making it possible for me to focus on my gifting and passions. Special thanks to Dr. B. Dale Taliaferro for his friendship and mentoring over the past twenty years. I will always admire and love you. Thanks also to Dr. Earl Radmacher for being an inspiration to all who know you to "fight the good fight."

I am grateful also for another friend who has been "closer than a brother," who always has my back, serves me, and serves with me. Thanks Jimbo!

Without the loving and enthusiastic nudging and partnership of the Van Diest duo, David & Sarah, this book may never have been written. If anybody reads it and enjoys the experience, much credit goes to Sarah. I have learned so much from you both. Thanks!

And thanks to all my family, especially my wife Angie who loves me and puts up with my all-or-nothing style in everything (especially in writing this book). And also my two wonderful boys, Carson and Cooper, who still think I am the greatest dad ever and whom I will always consider the best sons a father could have. I love you.

CONTENTS

FOREWORD

Many books on important subjects are written for the academic world in a sort of punch-counter-punch debate format, but few are ever written with similar depth for the average church member. This book is an exception to that practice, making it a must read for any student of the Bible. I am thankful that Curtis chose to write this book in such a way as to appeal and benefit all levels of interest and maturity.

Over a period of many years I have read nearly every book on the subject of the kingdom of God, but this one stands apart because it gripped and excited me like none other I have read. I must also admit that I have never read anything on the subject with such consistent development and interpretation. Let me say it again, no other book on this topic has kept me interested and excited like this one.

Majestic Destiny boldly reinforces the infinite love and matchless grace of God and revitalizes the Christian's hope in the returning of the Messiah. Great care and balance are given to difficult passages and concepts so that confusion and perceived conflict easily vanish.

The church has seriously diminished, or all but lost, the full biblical idea of Messianic Hope. In a pastor's conference at Moody, I presented the three tenses of salvation, which I first published in my book *Salvation,* where I suggested that many of us are saved and stuck rather than saved and saved and saved. Now, I didn't say saved and lost. Those who have been *saved* from the *penalty* of sin forever (justification salvation) need to go on being *saved* from the *power* of sin moment by moment (sanctification salvation), and the Messiah will be the ultimate deliverer of the world who will deal decisively and finally when we will be *saved* from sin's *presence* as well (glorification salvation).

That is the full sense of the title Messiah. Jesus Christ dealt with sin's penalty at the cross as the Suffering Servant, and is coming a second time in total triumph to reign supreme as King over the whole earth to fulfill all His promises, and His original intention for creation. The church must regain a full biblical perspective of Messiah so that hope may flourish and expand beyond just hoping for heaven after this life. Any discussion of Messianic hope must include the future reign of Christ upon this earth, because that is what we are looking forward to. This book will restore hope to the hopeless that we all "might with perseverance...wait eagerly for it" (Romans 8:25).

Without any hesitation whatsoever I recommend this book as a must read for all. It will grip you and motivate you to live *from* a place of assurance and security in God's love *for* His glory.

DR. EARL RADMACHER, TH.D.

PRESIDENT EMERITUS

WESTERN SEMINARY, PORTLAND, OR

PREFACE

Dissatisfaction is a worldwide epidemic.

Try to think of one people group or civilization, either present or in history, that found and was able to maintain any semblance of lasting peace, contentment, and satisfaction. You might come up with one or two examples that seem to hit on something good, but not a single tribe, nation, or people group has found it and sustained it.

Is that depressing to you? Do you wonder why we humans have failure written across the pages of our history?

Well, from a biblical perspective, it makes sense.

What were we created for? Was it to build great cities and invent marvelous machines? Was it to become an educated global community coming together to care for the earth? Was it to eat, drink, and be merry? Was it really for life, liberty, and the pursuit of happiness? Is democracy the answer?

Looking at the whole of mankind, we see that none of those goals have satisfied, even though we've gotten quite adept at striving for them and so many other things.

The bigger question is: Why did God get this whole ball rolling?

The thing we were created for is the thing we always strive after. Since time began, we have tried with all that is within us to make our kingdom. And not only do we want our kingdom, but we want our king to rule in such a way as we would like.

Because kingdom is what we are created for. Not for our kingdom, however, but God's.

Yet confusion over God's kingdom has led to great uncertainty and many misguided efforts. The traditional teachings of the Christian church have either led us to search for a new method to fix our world and make our own kingdom; or to hope only for the afterlife in heaven. We have changed or missed our purpose and misunderstood the true focus and emphasis of the Bible. We have been led to believe that there is nothing more to look forward to and nothing to live for...on this earth.

Heaven has become our highest aim. The hope and anticipation of the kingdom of God on earth has all but faded into nonexistence, as though that sun has set.

We are not in God's kingdom today.

We will not be able to realize God's kingdom through our own efforts.

But His kingdom is coming. Have no doubt.

And we must live for this kingdom, wait patiently for this kingdom, teach about this coming kingdom. We must set our sights upon this coming kingdom. The hope of His coming kingdom is rising!

And there is so much to live for.

For years I have seen lives changed when people grasp the clear distinction between heaven and the kingdom of Messiah. One is a gift and the other a prize. One must be received by faith alone, while the other, the prize, is earned through faithful obedience to God.

This book will draw those biblical distinctions and lead you along a path that resolves such debates as the existence of evil, how works are related to salvation, the eternal security of the believer, and the perseverance of the saints. This book will also help you find security in the matchless love and grace of our heavenly Father.

And equally important, this book will point you to a whole new orientation of life. The new orientation is toward the goal which God desires all of His children to share. It's the reason we were created and what mankind has yearned for: the coming kingdom of Christ.

But what about right now? Right now there is pain. Right now there is sorrow, grief, fighting, want, and depression. The world is full of injustice and heartache. How can we wait for the coming kingdom? How can we walk forward and endure? How can we persevere and finish the race? We are so tired; what's the point, anyway?

Despair not, for our Father has a wonderful plan. You know it in the depths of your heart. Creation itself longs for it (see Romans 8:18–25). You were created for something better than this world can give. You were created for something regal, something majestic. Be prepared, for God is going to undeniably, unequivocally show us, Satan, and all of creation who the real kingdom Maker is!

Journey with me as we walk through the Bible to find the truth that will give you what you need to persevere, so that you may walk into your majestic destiny and enter the joy of your King. The hope for His coming kingdom is rising.

Our King is coming!

ONE

SOUL SEARCHING

*What else does this craving, and this
helplessness, proclaim but
that there was once in man a true happiness, of which all that now remains
is the empty print and trace?*

Blaise Pascal

Millions of people around the world saw the movie *Avatar*. James Cameron gave people his view of a perfect kingdom in the portrayal of the moon Pandora– a pristine world not ruined by human greed and selfishness. It was visually spectacular.

It produced strong reactions from nearly everyone who saw it. But to the surprise of many, the strongest reactions were from people who experienced depression. Months after the premiere, CNN.com reported in an article entitled "Audiences Experience 'Avatar' Blues" that *Avatar* "may have been a little too real for some fans who say they have experienced depression and suicidal thoughts after seeing the film because they long to enjoy the beauty of the alien world Pandora."[1]

People walked out of the theater blown away by the unspoiled and wonderful world of Pandora, but as they reentered the reality of the world they actually lived in, they were thrust into despair.

Their reaction, if not justified, was at least understandable. Anyone who doesn't realize that this world is woefully short of paradise is living in a dream. And based upon history, we're not on the verge of creating it anytime soon. Except in the movies.

As this book is being written, Egypt is erupting in turmoil. In fact, the entire Middle East seems to be exploding in chaos. Every day brings new video footage of riots in the streets, people burning images of their leaders, and brutality of every sort. The basis for the upheaval is, simply put, that the people want a more just king and a better kingdom.

It's what we all want. It's what we long for. It's universal. We strive for it, fight for it, and sometimes people even die for it, but we never seem to attain it. It is always just outside our reach.

THE WORLD'S KINGDOM

When *The Times* invited several eminent authors to write essays on the theme "What's wrong with the world?" G. K. Chesterton responded by sending the editors this response:

> *Dear Sirs,*
>
> *I am.*
>
> *Sincerely yours,*
>
> *G. K. Chesterton*

Rather insightful of him, don't you think? This fact, which is universally true, has not changed. Our problem is that even though *"God made men upright...they have sought many devices."*[2]

The longing is good, but the methods we use and goals we seek are not.

William Temple, Archbishop of Canterbury from 1942–'44, was quoted as saying, "There is no structural organization of society which can bring about the coming of the Kingdom of God on earth, since all systems can be perverted by selfishness of man." Many people will run you down to get what they want; and if *they* don't, then the person behind them will. No amount of human, political, or even religious effort is going to resolve the issue.

It only takes a tour of your hometown with "eyes to see," or even a quick stroll through Wal-Mart, to glimpse the heavy burdens people carry and to realize that this world is seriously broken. No amount of big-screen TVs, beautiful buxom babes, or shiny BMWs is going to fix it. Neither will communism, socialism, or democracy. Yet we keep on seeking devices.

Divorce, revenge, and bitterness are symptoms of our longing for a better world—a world where we are happy, content, and satisfied. God has "made us upright" so we long for a kingdom to come that is good and ruled by a well-intentioned ruler, but we "seek many devices." The devices are our failed attempts at kingdom.

Just turn on your local news or take a look at the so-called reality TV and you will find every sort of selfish, unloving, uncaring act you can think of. But don't be surprised, because this is nothing new.

What *is* new today is that now we have twenty-four-hour cable news available to highlight it all and report it around the clock. There are now TV shows where the viewers watch as someone's car and other possessions are repossessed. Others entertain us with girls pulling each other's hair out over a guy or a broken cell phone. And then you have the punks (these come in both the girl and guy variety) beating up an innocent person just to post the video on YouTube.

It's no wonder depression, anxiety, and fear are at all-time highs. So onward we go seeking the next device, gimmick, trend, etc.

And we can look back in history to see the same sad story played out over and over again: ruthless dictators being overthrown by the oppressed only to have another equally evil tyrant take his place; hungry peasants revolting and establishing their own system of rule only to see starvation and corruption overtake them; kings battling for power and land, while sacrificing the lives of those they were meant to rule and protect.

This world's version of kingdom is doomed before it even begins.

This world's version of kingdom will never accomplish what we long for.

This world's schemes will never result in a kingdom that satisfies.

But take heart, because something far better is coming.

THE CHURCH'S KINGDOM

Is the church the answer to the mess of this world? Some would like us to think so. Are we simply not doing enough, not working hard enough, not being obedient enough?

Quite frankly, the pulse in the church is not a whole lot more promising than what we see in the world. The church is in a vicious cycle of searching and striving for something to attain, some goal to arrive at, a new gimmick to get us there. Each is altogether unrealistic and unbiblical.

This world's schemes will never result in a kingdom that satisfies.

The twentieth century provided a wide variety of church movements that began with Azusa Street Revivals, the spread of Pentecostalism, the press for fundamentalism, and the reaction of neo-evangelicalism. Yet over just the past thirty years, the evangelical church has been on a roller coaster of trends and fads, and the coaster is not slowing down one bit. Now the trends and gimmicks seem to come at record pace.

All of these trends, and those yet to be revealed, are the Christian man's way of seeking to answer the longing for something better. Every new church trend is their answer to the problem. This is the church's attempt at kingdom. We've busied ourselves with seeking solutions, and we always will. We strive and we strive!

But where has all this striving gotten us?

Are we any closer today than one hundred years ago?

No. All this striving has led to the next craze of church development and success. We see the trend of small groups, cell groups, and the house church movement. We see the shift from seeker-driven to seeker-sensitive, and then to the "purpose-driven church."

The big craze for years was the church growth movement, which gave way to the more recent "emerging church" movement and the "new apostolic reformation movement." And we now see the latest trends of liberation theology, new exodus movement, social justice, etc., etc., ad nauseam.

Just yesterday I read about another craze labeled "sustainable living" or what some have called the "Daniel Plan," which sure looks like a subtle adoption by some churches of the United Nations *Agenda 21*, which sees the resolution of all of our world problems in communal living and social justice. Another attempt at kingdom.

Are we kidding ourselves?

FALSE KINGDOMS

All of these, in one way or another, are feeble attempts to resolve the longing for something better. All of these trends are failed religious attempts at realizing the utopian goal we all crave. All of these in some form or fashion are religious attempts and striving for *kingdom now*. In many circles this is called kingdom dominion, or restoration theology, or whatever label you want to slap on the trend.

There is nothing new under the sun.

These trends and church fads are subtle attempts to realize the kingdom through our own effort. It is what has historically been called *postmillenialism* or *amillenialism*. In short, no future kingdom from Jesus; no hope of Jesus Christ's return to set up the kingdom He promised.

No kingdom of Messiah?

No dominion of Christ?

Then what's the point?

Nothing we have invented has worked thus far.

If this is true and there is no kingdom of the Messiah to look forward to, then it is all left up to us. And from the looks of it, we are in serious trouble! All of these failed attempts, trends, strategies, and so on rob us of our true hope (and our focus)!

No one is saying that we should not be concerned about world hunger, the AIDS epidemic, or impoverished countries...but the church is not going to solve world hunger. We are not going to resolve social justice, or save the planet by driving a Prius!

The church has a purpose and we need to be serious about that purpose. But it is not liberation theology, saving the planet, or solving world hunger. Our purpose is to remind people that a Savior died for them and promised to return to "[come] in His glory; and all the angels with Him, then He will sit on His glorious throne."[3]

Our King is coming.

The solution to the world's woes is the Christ who will return to reign supreme.

Nothing else will truly satisfy.

This kingdom plan of the Messiah is the central theme, the big idea, on the pages of the Bible. The big idea is not social reform or restoration, it is not sustainable living, and it is not about getting to heaven. You read that correctly...the big idea of the Bible is not about getting people to heaven. The big idea of the Bible is the coming kingdom of Christ.

We're looking for the fix, when in reality it—or I should say, "He"—has already come and is coming again. The King is coming to set up His kingdom on earth. The kingdom He is coming to set up will be the fulfillment of His great and glorious plan that began before the foundation of the world.[4]

God promised a kingdom on this earth, in time and space, and He will fulfill His promise. He promised it to Abraham, to David, and to Israel and He has never taken it away or yet fulfilled it.

GOD'S KINGDOM

The shocking reality for both the world and the church is: we're just looking in the wrong places.

That's right. What we all long for is already set to come...and it *is* coming.

A kingdom is coming that will blow all of our longings and desires right out of the water. I am talking about the second triumphant coming of Jesus Christ to set up His kingdom here upon this earth. His kingdom will be so amazing that it will make our utopian aspirations seem small-minded, sterile, and weak, to say the least.

The fact of the matter is that we've been chasing the perfect kingdom since the beginning of time. What we don't realize is that our efforts, no matter how well-intentioned, will always come up short regardless of how hard we try. "Vanity of vanities! All is vanity."[5]

God's kingdom is the kingdom everyone longs for because we were created for it. This kingdom which we were made for will be one of immense beauty and natural resources. Food will be plentiful and nutritious and won't make us fat (oh, how I look forward to this). There will be warmth and perfection that isn't fleeting and is not filled with the deteriorating effects of sin. Stress, anxiety, depression, and disease will all be things of the past. Satisfaction!

> *We were created for God's kingdom.*

In this kingdom, issues of disagreement (bickering, bitterness, revenge, fighting, jealousy, and greed) will be dealt with immediately and perfectly; amazingly enough, this is the kingdom where the lion will lie down with the lamb. And our King will rule justly, righteously, and with love, grace, and absolute power. His coming kingdom– a kingdom which will make the one portrayed in *Avatar* seem like a slum– will be worth the wait and the work.

Pascal concluded his observation of man's endless search to fill inner emptiness by stating that the "infinite abyss can be filled only with an infinite and immutable object; in other words by God himself."[6] God has a plan to reveal Himself and glorify Himself in the coming kingdom on earth that will connect at our very core.

THE JOURNEY TO THE KINGDOM

So come along as the pages of the Bible are opened to reveal God's wonderful plan. It's a plan that has far more to do with God's kingdom on earth than it has to do with getting to heaven or your salvation for eternity. We have to cease all of our tireless striving for something new to pacify our longing; and we must return to the ancient text to revive our pulse to the heartbeat of God...because He has a plan, and He wants to share it with you. In fact, He wants you to share and participate in it with Him!

Our first priority is to stop getting in our own way. Stop striving to attain what only God can bring. Stop trying to invent some alternative plan or method and slap some Christian-sounding label on it and ask God to bless it. Many today are corralling huge numbers of people into their church pens by using gimmicks and more, but we need to remember not to get caught up in the apparent success of it all. While these may seem to be great now, Jesus said that the "first will be last."[7] Appearance isn't everything.

Our hope is in the coming "kingdom of Christ and God,"[8] "the kingdom of His beloved Son"[9] "the eternal kingdom of our Lord and Savior."[10] It will be His "kingdom come [and His] will be done, on earth as it is in heaven."[11]

There is no true alternative. Nothing else will ever succeed or satisfy. The work we are doing today is preparatory work for this coming kingdom. The only things that matter are salvation by grace through faith alone, and our continual faithfulness for our inheritance (*our right to share!*) in the coming kingdom.

This idea of the kingdom resonates deep down in our very souls, because this is what we have been created for...and nothing short of His kingdom will satisfy! Nothing short of seeing Jesus Christ reign upon the earth will fill the longing in our souls.

Yes, it is going to take place on this earth!

And yes, it will satisfy!

NOTES

1 Jo Piazza, "Audiences Experience 'Avatar' Blues," CNN.com, January 11, 2010, http://articles.cnn.com/2010-01-11/entertainment/avatar.movie.blues_1_pandora-depressed-posts?_s=PM:SHOWBIZ.
2 Ecclesiastes 7:29
3 Matthew 25:31.
4 See Matthew 25:34.
5 Ecclesiastes 1:2.
6 Blaise Pascal, Pensees and Other Writings, trans. Honor Levi (Oxford: Oxford U.P., 1995), VII.
7 Matthew 19:30.
8 Ephesians 5:5.
9 Colossians 1:13.
10 2 Peter 1:11.
11 Matthew 6:10.

OUR FATHER'S LOVE

How deep the Father's love for us,
How vast beyond all measure
That He should give His only Son
To make a wretch His treasure.

Stuart Townend

Created for a kingdom and for a King to rule justly. So that's what I've been searching for? But what if I don't trust this so-called King? What if I don't really believe that this King to come has my best interest at heart? Or maybe I see Him as uncaring or distant. I certainly am not looking for that kind of king to rule over me.

Thankfully, that's not who our coming King is.

Jesus taught us to pray, "Our Father which art in heaven..."

The sheer magnitude of such a statement is almost too much to comprehend. God is a father? God is *"our"* father?

God is *my* Father?

Can this be true?

Yes, it is true...wonderfully true! The Bible says:

...as many as received Him, to them He gave the right to become children of God, even to those who believe in His name.[1]

Believing in Jesus Christ as our Savior makes us children of God, and so God is our Father.

But what kind of father is He?

Herein lies the rub! On one hand we know He must be the most trustworthy Father imaginable; yet on the other hand so many of us remain unsure, insecure, and even fearful of Him.

Those fears, insecurities, and doubts come from a fuzzy, blurred, and distorted picture of the Father. Cleaning up the picture we have of God should bring a sense of security, safety, motivation, and freedom to live a life for Him in the "fullness of joy."[2] If we're not experiencing the sense of being loved by Him, it's because our perspective of God is still lacking or muddled, and so we live in guilt, shame, insecurity, and fear.

Oh, but to know within your heart of hearts what is the "breadth and length and height and depth"[3] of the love of God!

A faulty, wrong, incomplete, poor, or fractured understanding of God will always lead to a faulty, wrong, incomplete, poor, or fractured experience of God. Our understanding of who He is doesn't change who He is, but it affects how we experience Him.

AN IMAGE OF GOD

How do you view God?

Do you think of God as an unhappy police officer on the hunt to "cuff and stuff" people who do wrong? Or an angry boss who constantly inspects work reviews to determine whom he can fire? Or an inspector at a border crossing who scrutinizes all your affairs to determine whether you come in or stay out?

Do you ever wonder if you are good enough for Him to love? Do you ever fear that your sins might cause Him to stop loving you? Or that He may change His mind about whether you can spend eternity with Him? Do you ever doubt God's love? Do you ever wonder if He is truly a committed, loving, caring, long-suffering God?

Do you ever think that you need to do good things so God will love you...*forever*?

If so, I speculate that this is probably due to some inaccurate biblical teaching you have received. So much inaccurate teaching is due to a failing on our part to make distinct what God says is distinct. There are lines that must be distinct.

Our guilt, shame, and fear can be resolved by simply distinguishing between the free gift of eternal salvation born out of God's eternal love and the plan He has for us: the plan He wishes to share with all those who love Him. The gift is relationship with Him, while the plan is His plan for the earth, which He has made our inheritance and wants to reward us with. When we adopt His plan we will realize our inheritance: the prize.

When passages that are intended to instruct us about the necessity of doing good works and being faithful to earn the *prize* are wrongly applied to the *gift,* then our view of a loving heavenly father is in serious jeopardy. This creates a negative downward spiral.

God puts no conditions on relationship with Him, but as a Father He must put conditions on rewards. If these two are kept distinct, this is what you get:

A God who loves the whole world and offers eternal salvation freely to all who believe. The gift has no strings attached; you don't have to do good works to earn it, prove you have it, or show you appreciate it.

A heavenly Father who knows how to motivate His kids to live for His glory by offering to reward us with great dividends in the inheritance He has planned for us.

A God who saves us by giving us a gift with no conditions, but motivates us to fulfill conditions by offering us reward.

If we maintain the distinction between the *gift* and the *prize,* and who that means God is, the result will be an awe-inspiring and accurate picture of our loving heavenly Father, the One who loves us unconditionally and has a wonderful plan for our lives.

A secondary benefit to maintaining this distinction is that many of the problems the church has wrestled with and divided over will be easily reconciled and resolved, and many of the passages that have troubled generations of God's kids will make sense.

SAVED BY GRACE ALONE

The Bible puts no conditions on God's love. So we must *stop* associating conditions, such as good works or perseverance, with God's love or with the gift of eternal salvation. Some of us don't even know that we do that—it's been so ingrained in us that we don't even see it.

Some say that to be truly saved, someone must repent, show remorse for what they've done, turn from every sin, commit their life to Christ, or that they must bear fruit. Some say that if someone goes back to their "wild ways," either they were never really saved to begin with or they lost their salvation. But God would never want you to live with that kind of insecurity, shame, guilt, or fear.

If works are necessary to earn, prove, or keep the gift, you will not comprehend or appreciate the love of the heavenly Father. You certainly won't feel the security you need to live for Him and fulfill the plan for which He created you.

> *Good works and grace are mutually esclusive.*

God loves you unconditionally. He does not need you to do anything for Him or prove anything to Him to be secure in His love. That is grace!

Good works and grace are mutually exclusive!

But God does have big plans for us. This is where the good works and perseverance come in. The good works are always a condition we must meet in order to realize the plan He has for us *for the prize*!

This gets at the very core of His wonderful plan.

THE WONDERFUL PLAN: THE KINGDOM

"Hallowed be Your name. Your kingdom come...on earth as it is in heaven."[4]

God's plan is a kingdom plan.

God wants His name to be made holy and therefore wants us to be faithful, to do good works by faith, for the prize. The prize is our inheritance, the rewards, in the coming kingdom of God; it's His plan.

The topic of rewards has little effect on many people; this is in large part because of the mistaken teaching that rewards find fulfillment in heaven. So the idea that most people seem to have is that if there are rewards, then it's something like getting lots of jewels in your crown in heaven, which you wear while you enjoy an everlasting worship service.

And for many people heaven is like a fog. As Bruce Wilkinson states, "If you are like most people you picture eternity [heaven] somewhat like a West Texas highway—flat, long and monotonous."[5]

In reality, the Bible speaks very little about heaven, so we don't know much about it. Attaching rewards to heaven has made us very negligent about them. We just think, "What's the big deal? Heaven's going to be great...why do I care if I even *get* a crown, much less how many jewels I get in it?" But that's not the correct picture. We've got it all wrong.

Our rewards don't apply to heaven at all. They apply to the kingdom!

While we do "lay up" rewards in heaven (*for now*) and will receive the rewards in heaven at the judgment seat of Christ, the application of the rewards has nothing to do with heaven in their fulfillment or use. Rewards will be used for the kingdom.

The kingdom is what God is planning for at the culmination of history. This is His plan.

That is why Jesus taught us to pray, "Thy kingdom come... in earth, as it is in heaven,"[6] and why He said to "seek first His kingdom."[7]

The wonderful plan He has for us is His kingdom plan for this earth. Our future participation in the coming kingdom is totally dependent upon how we live for the glory of our heavenly Father today.

Read that again: *Our **participation in the kingdom** is totally dependent upon how we live for the glory of our heavenly Father.*

That is the wonderful plan!

Our salvation does not guarantee us our full inheritance in the coming kingdom of Christ, although our "ability" to enter the coming kingdom is dependent upon our eternal salvation![8]

The fact that God saved us guarantees our eternal salvation and our eternal connection to Him, on the basis of His character (not ours). That relationship cannot be broken or interrupted, for He would never leave us or forsake us.[9]

The rewards, on the other hand, come only by faithfulness to Him. For "without faith it is impossible to please Him, for he who comes to God must believe that He is and that He is a rewarder of those who seek Him."[10]

When we are unfaithful (and we all know this is possible!), He will discipline us because He loves us,[11] and He does not want us to lose heart[12] in the wonderful plan He has for us. That is what a heavenly Father does. Yet He will never discipline us by taking away the gift.[13] He will never cease to love you.[14] He will never hold the gift over your head! And He will never take the gift back or give up on you!

We can't move forward to the reward unless we know that we stand saved[15] and have been "rooted and grounded in love."[16]

Maintaining this distinction between the gift and the prize, between eternal salvation and the coming kingdom of God on earth, should restore to you a clear and truthful perspective of a loving heavenly Father; it should give you all the motivation you need to live for His glory and pursue the wonderful plan He has for you.

It is liberating!

He is a loving Father who desires to reward, not a Father who rewards with His love.

> *He is a loving Father who desires to reward.*

A REAL LIFE COMPARISON

My wife, Angie, and I have two boys whom we love unconditionally. Our commitment to them is that regardless of what they do, whether good or bad, we will always love them and be their parents. Our boys also know very well that if they do wrong there are consequences, and if they do what is right they can expect to be rewarded. But our love to them is constant; our love is never a reward or remuneration. They will always and forever be "Tucker boys" no matter what they do.

Rewards are important, but are never linked to a parent's love... this is the story of the Bible!

The gift is a result of God's love and is unconditional. The prize is why He continues to develop us, help us grow up, chasten us when we get off track, prune us when we are sagging and not bearing fruit—to gain the fullness of our inheritance and fulfill our purpose.

He wants all to receive the gift and become His kids so He can be a Father to them. And He wants to lovingly father us all to fulfill the plan for which He created us.

This plan of His, then, must become our purpose.

NOTES

1 John 1:12.
2 Psalm 16:11.
3 Ephesians 3:17–19.
4 Matthew 6:9–10.
5 Bruce Wilkinson, *A Life God Rewards* (Sisters, Ore.: Multnomah Publishers, 2002), 19.
6 Matthew 6:10, KJV.
7 Matthew 6:33.
8 John 3:3, 5.
9 See Hebrews 13:5.
10 Hebrews 11:6.
11 See Hebrews 12:5–10.
12 See Hebrews 12:3.
13 See John 10:28–30.
14 See Romans 8:35, 39.
15 Ephesians 2:5, 8.
16 Ephesians 3:17.

THREE

PICTURE
OF PURPOSE

*A ship is safe in harbor, but that's not
what ships are for.*
William Shedd

Every human being has a deep inner longing for meaning,
significance, and purpose. For some, these three may be
distinct; but even if distinct, they are inextricably tied together.

- What is the meaning of life?

- Am I significant?

- What, if any, should be my purpose?

The answers to questions of meaning, significance, and purpose
are found in the all-sufficient Creator God.

If you want to find out why something was created, then you
must consult the maker of the thing, not the thing. The thing
doesn't possess the capacity to understand or know the thoughts of

its maker on its own. So, in order to find out why man was created, his creator is the one to turn to, not to man himself.

The purpose for which God created becomes the purpose of the created.

Read that again: *The purpose for which God created becomes the purpose of the created.*

Doesn't that make sense? Why did the cobbler make a shoe? Because he needed something to keep his feet from being cut and bruised. And what is the purpose of a shoe? To keep feet from being cut and bruised. Why did the baker make bread? To feed someone who was hungry. And what is the purpose of bread? To satisfy someone's hunger.

We get it wrong when we say that the purpose of a shoe is to look good, or the purpose of bread is to smell good. Those attributes may be true, but they aren't the purpose for which the item was created.

So then, why did God make you? Maybe you look good and smell good, but that is not your purpose.

Many books have been written that correctly recognize that the basis for personal purpose is found in God. The recent highly acclaimed book Purpose Driven Life by author and pastor Rick Warren has been called a "groundbreaking manifesto on the meaning of life." We read in the opening chapter, "You must begin with God. You were born by his purpose and for his purpose."[1]

As Warren states, "It is only in God that we discover our origin, our identity, our meaning, our purpose, our significance, and our destiny. Every other path leads to a dead end."[2] On this much we agree.

But while Warren offers his own perspective on God's five purposes for each of us—real worship, real fellowship, real discipleship, real ministry, and real evangelism—we should ask ourselves whether these are really purposes at all.

The word purpose is defined as "the object toward which one strives or for which something exists: goal."[3] It would seem very limited in scope if we were to reason that God's purpose is for us to perform certain practices with no greater goal than the mere accomplishment of those practices.

It is a slippery slope into a religious rut if we allow any practice to become our purpose, for that undoubtedly limits us to a performance-based existence. Our heavenly Father has bigger things in mind for us than mere religious performances. Under this performance prescription we are headed down a road that has danger written all over it! The signs ahead will often read Guilt, Shame, Failure, and Fear. This all goes back to our perspective of the heavenly Father. The practices are a means to an end, not the end!

Practices in themselves are not bad; what determines their value is what goal you attach to the practices. If the goal is heaven or eternity with God, we slip into thinking that God's commitment to us is dependent upon our performance of the practice, our perseverance.

Remember, the Bible makes it clear that our eternal destiny is a gift given by God that we receive by faith without works.[4] The guarantee of the gift is related to the character of the Giver, not the recipient.

God's character, not ours, guarantees the security of our eternal relationship with the Father.

PARADIGM SHIFT

So why do we find ourselves so often back here struggling with guilt, shame, and inadequacy? Why can't we accept that our performance doesn't impact or influence God's verdict about us? It is because we have blurred lines that need be distinct.

It's like talking with an ancient astronomer and trying to convince him that the earth is not the center of the universe. Though many Muslim astronomers had come up with almost identical lunar calculations to Copernicus's, even prior to his life, they weren't able to make the paradigm shift to allow for the concept of the earth orbiting around something else. The evidence was there, but their beliefs, supported by Islamic tradition, held them too tightly to allow them to see the truth.

In the same way, we have the evidence in Scripture. We have all the information, but we just can't make the paradigm shift to see the truth; we don't seem able to understand what the lunar calculations are telling us.

Here's what I mean:

From Genesis to Revelation, the main theme of the Bible is the coming kingdom of Christ. It's not salvation. It's not heaven. It's not forgiveness or grace, or even eternity. It's the millennial reign of Christ, the total theocratic dominion we all long for.

> *From Genesis to Revelation, the main theme of the Bible is the kingdom.*

There is a distinction in Scripture between God's plan for eternity and His glorious plan for the ages of history (in time), but we fail to see the two as distinct: eternal salvation and the millennial reign of Christ in the kingdom of God on earth.

So, we take all of those Scriptures that talk about how faith without works is dead, how we must work out our salvation, take up our cross, hate our own life, the rich young ruler, the Sermon on the Mount, fear of not entering rest spoken of in Hebrews, and how certain ones characterized by a lifestyle of sin "won't inherit the kingdom"...and we misapply them.

We declare that these passages, and others like them, refer to our eternal salvation because we don't know that it's an option for the earth to orbit the sun...or rather, that the Scriptures might apply to something other than our eternal salvation: the millennial reign of Christ, the kingdom of God on earth.

God loves us because He is love. We, His creatures, are the object of His affections because we have been created for His purpose. His purpose is not to fill heaven with a slew of believers; it is to develop a kingdom of priests to use for His glory in the coming kingdom of Messiah. When we arrive with our full reward, God will receive the glory. We will be His trophies![5] That is why His plan is important... why rewards are so important.

This is the reason we are on this earth. This is the end to which God is calling and choosing us.[6] Doing good works by faith is the way we fulfill the obligation that comes along with our calling and appointment; it is part of God's wonderful plan. This is how God is working today to make us trophies of His glory and grace now and in the age to come.[7]

We cannot be so farsighted (looking to eternity) that we miss why we are here on earth.

God created the earth and all it contains for the establishment of His kingdom in order to bring final defeat to His archenemy, the devil. This is what God is doing and what He wants us to become so His glory will shine through us.

The work that Jesus did was kingdom work.

The incredible price He paid on the cross is what provides our access to His riches. Make no mistake, the work He will finish will be kingdom work.

All of history points toward the kingdom.

We exist for the very same purpose, from which God will be glorified.

This is why it is so important for us to pursue, search, and strive for His kingdom and what is right.[8]

The kingdom on earth, as pastor and author Stu Weber commented, is "the fulfillment of the Father's dream on this planet among human beings—his kingdom realized on earth as it is in heaven"[9]

This is what the Father has to share with us...this is the reason we are created.

This is His wonderful plan.

WHEN WE HAVE "THE WHY"

We are His children, created and saved for His plan and purpose (all for His glory).

As Nietzsche said, "He who has a why to live can bear almost any how." We have the why: the glory of God as it is revealed in His glorious plan for the ages. The why of His purpose ought to change and sustain the how, the way you live.

My family recently discovered a newfound purpose in quarters, dimes, nickels, and even pennies that is radically affecting the way we think about spare change. I brought home an empty five-gallon bottle from our office water cooler. As a family, we discussed how great it would be if we could fill the bottle with change and use the money to take a really nice family vacation.

Immediately, the whole family was onboard.

We had a shared purpose.

Since the inception of this new purpose, we have newfound enthusiasm about saving change. It is exciting to drop a handful of coins into the bottle. Prior to our little plan, I was in the habit of leaving spare change in a careless manner. Rather than break a bill, I would ransack my car's ashtray to pay for something (to the chagrin of those behind me in the fast food drive-through). But no longer.

The only reason for this fundamental shift in our "changed paradigm" is purpose. Having a clear and defined purpose is changing our lifestyle.

In our spiritual lives, we can bear any how once we understand the why. We don't do good works to prove anything to anyone, or to stay in God's good graces, or to secure our salvation. We work toward that for which we were created and saved: God's glorious plan.

In the words of Vince Lombardi, "Success demands singleness of purpose." Our purpose is to glorify God, whose glory will be displayed to the greatest degree in the coming kingdom of Messiah.

We must be as kingdom minded as He is in order to truly live for His glory.

NOTES

1 Rick Warren, *A Purpose Driven Life* (Grand Rapids, MI: Zondervan, 2004), 17.

2 Ibid., 18.

3 *Webster's New College Dictionary*, 11th ed. (Springfield, MA: Merriam-Webster, 2003), s.v. "purpose."

4 See Ephesians 2:8–9; Romans 4:4–5.

5 See Ephesians 2:7.

6 See 2 Peter 1:10.

7 See Ephesians 1:12, 14, 18; 2:7.

8 See Matthew 6:33.

9 Stu Weber, Holman New Testament Commentary: Matthew (Nashville, TN: B&H Publishing Group, 2000), 6.

FOUR

BIRD'S-EYE VIEW

If you do not raise your eyes you will think that you are the highest point.
Antonio Porchia

In the late 1990s, I had the privilege of learning to fly an airplane in my training to become a private pilot (a goal I fell ten hours short of...*for now*). One of the most fascinating and enjoyable things about flying a small airplane was the perspective of what lies below. I have always had a good sense of direction and a decent grasp on the lay of the land; but at a thousand feet in the air, my whole perspective and appreciation for the landscape changed.

I could understand with great clarity the relation of one landmark to another, the orientation of roads and highways, the layout of city streets, the bend in a river, etc. In fact, I would often get so enamored with surveying the landscape that it was a challenge just to remember to fly the plane.

There really is something special in a bird's-eye view.

In the church today, much of what has been taught and learned has sadly led us to miss the main point in the Bible. We have become so engrossed in the details that we can't see the big idea of what God is doing in His creation. The traditional mind-set within the church has been to focus on the old dichotomy of heaven and hell.

But that is not the big idea on the pages of Scripture.

Let's hover over this idea and take in the entire landscape.

FROM BEGINNING TO ENDING, AND BEYOND

The beginning of time is simply that, the beginning of time. That statement implies two things: 1) before time began, there was the absence of time and 2) if time had a beginning, then it will have an ending. See the timeline on the opposite page and note the three major things that also have a beginning and an ending: the earth, Hades/hell/the grave, and heaven. But contrary to what our linear minds tend to allow, there is still more to come following the ending of time: the New Heaven and the New Earth, and the Lake of Fire. Those exist outside of time and within eternity.

Things which exist within the confines of time are finite. Heaven, for example, is finite. The grave is finite. And the millennial kingdom, which is a thousand-year period (finite), is the culmination of all time in which the fullness of the glory of God is revealed to the whole earth and time will sing His praises. Only after His earthly reign will Christ "[hand] over the kingdom to the God and Father;"[1] and then His reign will continue throughout all eternity.

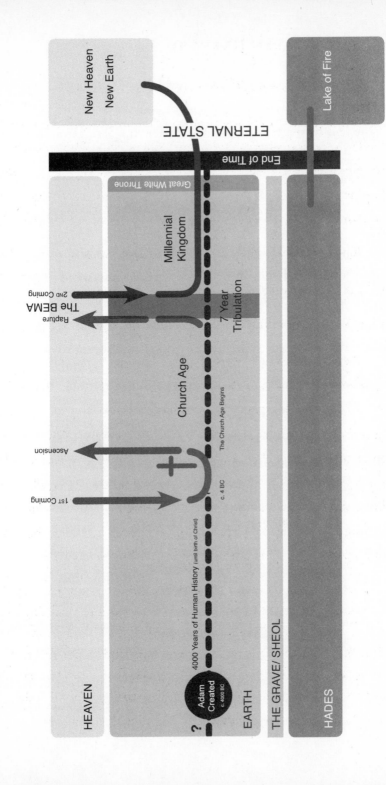

But, it is this millennial kingdom, this thousand-year reign of Christ on earth, which dominates the pages of Scripture. And that is the lens through which we are to view the Scriptures. Without these glasses, we misunderstand, misinterpret, and even mistranslate the Bible.

KINGDOM PERSPECTIVE AND SALVATION

When we look simply at what Scripture says and realize that it's all about God's kingdom, we can better understand important doctrinal issues such as salvation. The questions that so many struggle with regarding the security of their salvation are resolved when we allow the Scripture to say what it was meant to say.

The solid student of the Bible must know not only the issues covered within the pages of Scripture but also how to connect those issues. For example, one may discern that a doctrine of perseverance is discussed in the Bible; but if perseverance is attached to the doctrine of **justification** (meaning that it's our perseverance that eternally saves us or proves we are saved) instead of **sanctification** or **glorification**, then biblical instruction gets hopelessly clouded.

> ### Salvation in Three Phases
>
> **Justification.** Salvation from sin's penalty: a free and unconditional gift received by grace through faith alone.
> **Sanctification.** Salvation from sin's power: happens only by the power of the Holy Spirit as the justified walk by faith.
> **Glorification.** Salvation from sin's presence and the glorified rewarded to share in His glory.

It's like saying that people who walk according to the flesh and "practice such things"[2] prove by their lack of perseverance in holy conduct that they have either lost their salvation or were never genuinely saved. But Paul says that those who "practice such things will not inherit the kingdom of God."[3] Inheriting the kingdom is about glorification, not justification. Thus our sanctification ("[walking] by the Spirit"[4]) is effecting our glorification, not our justification.

Isn't that crystal clear? When we look at it with the understanding that inheritance in the kingdom is a reward, the prize, then it makes sense that someone who doesn't act rightly forfeits their share in that reward. But it doesn't change their standing before God as saved or not saved, nor does it indicate that they never believed in the first place.

One would think that after two thousand years of study, the church would have reached an agreement over the issue of salvation. Unfortunately, and sadly, this is not the case.

ALL WE SEE IS THE TREE

Henry C. Thiessen, in his Lectures in Systematic Theology, said of salvation, "In no field are there more differences of opinion and in no study are the conclusions more far-reaching."[5] Many different theological schools and even more local churches have fed this confusion by making salvation simply about "getting to heaven."

Others have erred in identifying the kingdom of heaven with heaven itself (or with salvation), missing the big idea of the Bible altogether. But these distinctions make all the difference in how we see our Christian walk and are critical to our spiritual lives. As one gentleman wrote to me:

I now know that salvation is my freedom from fear, freedom from sin, and through growth I can have power over sin with a goal of completing His will now, and for my place in the future kingdom! Simply knowing and grasping the word salvation instead of just hearing it over and over, without substance, changed my life!

Mike M.

Eternal salvation from the penalty of sin is what the Bible calls justification: being declared righteous on the basis of Christ's righteousness attributed to us. Yet justification is not the only salvation of the Bible.

Another aspect of salvation is the salvation that justified children of God can experience from sin's power as we walk by faith. This salvation is called sanctification.

The final aspect of salvation is a future time of salvation when God's children will be saved from sin's presence as they receive a body without sin[6] and are given rewards to be enjoyed in the glorious earthly reign of Christ; the kingdom. This is called glorification.

The church has overemphasized the first aspect of salvation (justification) and mistakenly made eternal salvation synonymous with heaven and the kingdom. Exacerbating this mistake, many have mistakenly tried to answer questions about the relationship of good works within the discussion of justification by grace through faith apart from works.

But in reality, obedience to God and good works prove kingdom worthiness, not eternal worth.

OUR NEW VANTAGE POINT

So, from your new mile-high perspective, are you beginning to get the lay of the land? Do you see how the roads connect and where they lead? By understanding that the Bible's main emphasis is on the coming kingdom, we can see the Scriptures as they were intended; we can begin to unravel the passages that have caused us such consternation and confusion.

> *Obedience to God and good works prove kingdom worthiness, not eternal worth.*

Jesus commanded His specifically called and appointed disciples to "seek first His kingdom and His righteousness."[7] With this new perspective, we can easily identify that Jesus is actually talking about the coming kingdom, not some ethereal version of kingdom or analogy for heaven.

This kingdom is something we must seek; it is something we must strive for. And our efforts, when done in faith, produce His righteousness and will result in our reward and the glory of God magnified. For the glory of our Father is what this is all about!

NOTES

1 1 Corinthians 15:24.
2 Galatians 5:21.
3 Ibid., emphasis added.
4 Galatians 5:16.
5 Henry C. Thiessen, *Lectures in Systematic Theology,* rev. ed. (Grand Rapids, MI: Wm. B. Eerdmans Publishing Company, 1979), 201.
6 See Philippians 3:21; 1 Corinthians 15:42–43, 49
7 Matthew 6:33.

FIVE

FOR HIS GLORY

Mine eyes have seen the glory of the coming of the Lord.

Julia Ward Howe

E verything that exists is created for His glory.

An ocean shoreline receiving thunderous waves, majestic mountain peaks covered in shimmering snow, stars that shine in the heavens. All this and more was created for His glory, for "the heavens are telling of the glory of God; and their expanse is declaring the work of His hands."[1] In fact, everything on earth was and is created for His glory.

And so are we.

The Scripture says, "Everyone who is called by My name, and whom I have created for My glory, whom I have formed, even whom I have made."[2]

God created for the purpose of being glorified.

The cobbler made the shoe for the purpose of protecting his foot, and likewise the Father made us for the purpose of bringing Him glory. So the mantra of our lives is "whatever you do, do all to the glory of God."[3] For glorifying God is at the very heart of our purpose; it is always the goal.

We are God's trophies.

But we struggle sometimes with understanding what it means to bring God glory. Simply put, to glorify God is to make His attributes known. In his commentary on the book of Ephesians, Harold Hoehner says, "Glory is the essence of one's being, the summation of all of one's attributes"[4] Thus, to give God glory is to make His attributes known.

It's like this: when a runner wins a race, he gets a trophy. That trophy tells everyone who sees it that he has the ability to run really fast. The trophy is a symbol of the glory awarded him because of his speed. Simple.

We are God's trophies. This is clearly seen in a number of passages. Here are a few:

"(By grace you have been saved) and raised up with Him, and seated with Him in the heavenly places in Christ Jesus, so that in the ages to come He might show the surpassing riches of His grace in kindness toward us in Christ Jesus."[5]

"He predestined us to adoption as sons...to the praise of the glory of His grace."[6]

"We who were the first to hope in Christ would be to the praise of His glory."[7]

Our purpose is to show how amazing a Creator, Father, Savior, Lover, Rescuer, Redeemer, Helper, Sustainer, and Comforter He is. And the more trophies there are, the more glowing will be the greatness of His glory. This is true today in small measure, but one day it will be true in majestic proportions. It is the glory that creation longs for.[8]

The glory of God is going somewhere; it has direction. While God's glory has been and is revealed in varying degrees, the greatest degree of His glory is yet to come!

We are on display today, but the trophy case is in the age to come.

This story of God's glory has been in process since the beginning.

PAST: GOD'S GLORY REVEALED IN CREATION

In the beginning God worked for six days, the result of which was the entire inhabitable universe and all that it contains.[9] "It was good."[10]

What was created by Him reveals His glory. The mere majesty and beauty, as well as the natural order that exists in creation, reveal His dominion, sovereignty, and power. The glory of God is evident in the constellations, the sun, the moon, the oceans, and even the tiniest sparrow.

Modern scientists call the glory of natural order the anthropic principle, which asserts that the universe was constructed within very narrow limits in such a way that man could dwell in it. If that structure and order is changed in the slightest, life could not exist.

Glory to God in the highest.

Despite the telling nature of nature itself, man ignores this clear evidence of God's glory and chooses "a lie, and [worships] and [serves] the creature rather than the Creator."[11] The glory in creation is not foolproof, but boy howdy does it give glory some visual substance!

C. S. Lewis said, "Nature never taught me that there exists a God of glory and of infinite majesty. I had to learn that in other ways. But nature gave the word glory a meaning for me."[12]

Everything in creation reveals God's glory and gives His glory meaning as He intended.[13]

Though nature and all we see and marvel at in creation is awe-inspiring, man displays God's glory at a new level. The glory of the Father was ratcheted up a notch when He created man.

While man was formed from dust, he was created in the likeness of God.[14] Nothing else in creation can boast any such thing. Not only is man made in the image of his Creator; his Creator performed a unique life-giving operation by breathing life directly into him.[15]

Man is the masterpiece of God's creative work and he did not evolve from fish or apes. He was created by the God of all glory.

"It was very good!"[16]

David celebrated God's glory in man when he said, "I will give thanks to You, for I am fearfully and wonderfully made; wonderful are Your works, and my soul knows it very well."[17] Everything about man is a revelation of God's glory. The flutter of an eyelid to keep out dust, the slight twist of blood vessels so blood will flow more smoothly, the uniqueness in a single person's fingerprint, the complex workings of the retina, and the distinctiveness of an individual personality—all reveal God's glorious handiwork and genius.

The glory of God is clearly evident in man.

We truly are fearfully and wonderfully made.

To God be the glory!

GLORY REVEALED IN HISTORY

God did not cease to reveal His glory after creation. Think of miracles throughout history—times where God intervened and was glorified. It may have been as simple as a voice in the Garden[18] or as phenomenal as a bush that blazed but did not burn.[19] These are examples of God Himself showing up for man to witness personal manifestations of His glory.

God glorified Himself in many ways in the Old Testament:

through a pillar of cloud or fire, plagues, parting of large bodies of water, manna from heaven, and acts of kindness toward man.[20] Historically, however, the most consistent display of His glory was the constant abiding presence of the Shekinah dwelling in the Most Holy Place. While that Shekinah Glory departed the temple[21] because of the disobedience of the nation of Israel, the promise of His return in even greater glory remains.[22]

This promise gives us a foretaste of future glory!

After a four-hundred-year absence of God's abiding glory, a child was born to a virgin in the town of Bethlehem, as had been promised seven hundred years prior.[23] As it is said, "There is much in a name." The name of that child tells it all: it was God with us.[24]

God's glorious workings once again took center stage. That glory of the unique member of the godhead was beheld by those living in that day.[25] The author of Hebrews adds that Jesus' glory was reflective glory of the Father.[26] Jesus displayed great glory in His works, but it was not yet the greatest. His own glory was veiled in His humanity.

On two occasions, however, Jesus gave a glimpse of His majestic glory. Once was with the disciples[27]; and later, the Roman guard in the Garden.[28]

It was not until Jesus was crucified and resurrected that it was said that "He was glorified"[29] with the glory He had before, which He had veiled when He came to live and die for all mankind.[30] Yet even at the point of death and resurrection, it is not yet His greatest degree of glory He has planned to display.

PRESENT: GOD'S GLORY TODAY

While creation continues to reveal the glory of God, the church is presently the main instrument through which the glory of God is being revealed.[31] Christ is glorified as the church grows and is transformed to walk in a holy manner.[32]

Each individual, as a member of the body of Christ, can make a difference and play an important part in the present work of glory. Despite our human imperfections, God's glory is being revealed through the expression of new life, which we have been given on the basis of grace through faith.[33]

As the Holy Spirit empowers the child of God, the very life of Jesus Christ shines through our practical righteousness and God gets glory.[34] This is true because the life lived by faith expresses the very life of Christ.[35] Thus, it is a revelation of His attributes.

I have the privilege of knowing a dear friend and brother in Christ named Steve. Steve is now in his fifties, but a number of years ago he was an alcoholic in the worst sense of the word. He drank himself right into the hospital and was on his deathbed. The doctors told him it was only a matter of days before he died. But God did something wonderful and special.

While lying on his deathbed, God revealed Himself in dramatic fashion. Right then and there, Steve believed in Christ and was eternally saved and received the Holy Spirit. His physical life was spared and his life changed forever. Many years now removed from that hospital bed and his imprisonment to alcoholism, he lives passionately loving God and others.

Every time I see him, the glory of God shines.

When we live for God's glory, not our own, God is glorified

When we live by the power of the Holy Spirit and we reveal the life of Christ in us, God is glorified.

While this is truly remarkable, and something which I never tire of seeing, it too is limited, for there is greater glory still to be seen.

The greatest degree of glory of Jesus Christ is that which we are eagerly awaiting: when He returns triumphantly to set up His kingdom.[36]

FUTURE: GLORY TO BE REVEALED

The greatest revelation of God's glory is yet to come. It is yet future. This time of future glory will be a time when the full summation of His attributes are known by all. "Now I know in part, but then I will know fully."[37]

> *The greatest revelation of God's glory is yet to come.*

Today some deny His very existence, but there is a fixed time in the future when His presence will be undeniable.[38] It will be a time when every nation, race, and tongue will see and declare His glory.[39] As the prophet Habakkuk said, "The earth will be filled with the knowledge of the glory of the LORD, as the waters cover the sea."[40]

This will be the most pervasive, powerful, and prominent display of the glory of God.

It will be the personal presence of the glorious King that elicits worldwide worship.[41]

GOING DEEPER

John Walvoord commented on the glory of Messiah in the coming kingdom when he wrote: "the glory of the humanity of Christ is manifested in His glorious dominion...a glorious government...a glorious inheritance of the Promised Land...a glorious prophet and lawgiver... a glorious house and throne fulfilling the Davidic covenant...and the glory of the kingdom itself..."

and to "...the glory of Christ as it pertains to His deity...omniscience... and omnipotence...are revealed in the Millennium...as God He receives worship...other attributes, and divine qualities manifested in the Millennial reign of Christ are righteousness...divine mercy...divine goodness...and holiness...and divine truth..."

There is no mistaking that the first coming did not accomplish tis extent of glory, nor does His present ministry as head over the church. [42]

The coming future kingdom "will be the period of the full manifestations of the glory of the Lord Jesus Christ."[43] It must be this way, for "it does appear *eminently proper* that the theatre of King Jesus' humiliation, sufferings, and death *should witness also* His exaltation and glory...when Christ shall be *openly and visibly recognized* as the glorious One."[44]

The future plan of God will undoubtedly be an unmatched display of the glory of God. We are not presently in the glorious kingdom of the Glorious One. The only conceivable solution to such revelation is that this glorious display is yet future.

God will wrap up history in this glorious fashion.

In the book of Acts, the coming kingdom is appropriately called "THE GREAT AND GLORIOUS DAY OF THE LORD."[45] It will be at that time when the "Branch of the LORD will be beautiful and glorious."[46] His glory will be so great it will outshine the moon and the sun,[47] and will be visible to all.[48] There has never been, nor will there ever be, such a display of glory until the glorious kingdom of Messiah.

This is the direction God's glory is headed! This is what God is doing and what He has created us to share in.

If we truly accept that our purpose is to glorify God, how then should we live? It's easy for the shoe to "live" according to its purpose, as it has no ability to go outside of its created purpose on its own. But we do.

LOOKING UNTO JESUS

The writer of Hebrews compares life to a race and tells us to "run with endurance the race that is set before us."[49] The metaphor of a race and running makes little sense unless we see the explanation given by the author concerning *how we are to run*.

It's simple, really. We run by looking. Imagine running at full speed with your eyes closed, or while staring at your shoes, or with your eyes on your iPod! The outcome of each of these would be less than pleasant, and the goal of getting to where you were trying to run would likely not be accomplished.

We must turn our eyes away from everything that distracts and deters us, and turn our full attention upon Jesus.[50] For "truth is in Jesus,"[51] and He alone is the "Light of the world."[52] *Looking* in the spiritual world is like moving your legs in the physical world. Looking is trusting! Looking is following.

Jesus is the first to go down the path. He is the pioneer and also the one who brings our faith to its highest achievements.[53] If we want to live for the glory of God, we simply need to look to Jesus.

While Jesus was on earth He did nothing that did not first originate with His Father,[54] and He was confident and focused on the glorious plan.[55]

What a leader He is for us.

He blazed the trail and cut the path for us to follow.

When we look to Jesus, we will manifest His life today. We will be transformed into His image, that we might be glorified with Him.[56] This will bring great glory to God.

When we are transformed into His image, we are being prepared for the ages to come that we might share in His glory[57] and exist as trophies to display His glory.[58]

Living now prepares us for the glorious kingdom to come.

Our participation in the coming kingdom will be for the glory of God.

As that runner received a trophy to showcase his ability to run quickly, in the coming kingdom we are to be the trophies of God, highlighting how majestic, gracious, and marvelous He is. How humbling, exciting, motivating, and inspiring it is to think that each of us could shine as a trophy, giving glory to our heavenly Father in the coming kingdom!

NOTES

1 Psalm 19:1.

2 Isaiah 43:7.

3 1 Corinthians 10:31.

4 Harold Hoehner, *Ephesians, An Exegetical Commentary* (Ada, MI: Baker Academic, 2002), 255.

5 Ephesians 2:5–7.

6 Ephesians 1:5–6.

7 Ephesians 1:12.

8 See Romans 8:19.

9 It may be that God created the mass of heaven and earth (Genesis 1:1) many eons prior to His six days of creation (Genesis 1:2–31). If that is true, then the six days is taking what was previously made and making it habitable for man.

10 Genesis 1:4, 10, 12, 18, 21, 25.

11 Romans 1:23, 25.

12 C. S. Lewis, *The Four Loves* (New York: Houghton Mifflin Harcourt, 1991), 20.

13 See Psalm 19:1.

14 See Genesis 1:26–27; 2:7.

15 See Genesis 2:7b.

16 Genesis 1:31.

17 Psalm 139:14.

18 See Genesis 3:8–9.

19 See Exodus 3:2.

20 See Exodus 33:18.

21 See Ezekiel 9:3–11:23.

22 See Ezekiel 43:1–5.

23 See Luke 2:4; Isaiah 7:14; Micah 5:2.

24 See Isaiah 7:14b.

25 See John 1:14.

26 See Hebrews 1:3.

27 See Luke 9:32.

28 See John 18:1–11.

29 See John 7:9; 12:16, 23, 28; 13:31–32.

30 See John 17:5; Philippians 2:6–8.

31 See Ephesians 3:21.

32 See Ephesians 5:27.

33 See John 3:3, 5, 15–16.

34 See Galatians 2:20; Colossians 3:4.

35 See Galatians 2:20.

36 See Matthew 25:31.

37 1 Corinthians 13:12.

38 See Isaiah 11:9.

39 See Isaiah 66:18b–19.
40 Habakkuk 2:14.
41 See Isaiah 66:23; Philippians 2:9–11.
42 John Walvoord, *The Millennial Kingdom: A Basic Text in Premillennial Theology* (Grand Rapids, MI: Zondervan Publishers, 1983), 306–7.
43 J. Dwight Pentecost, *Things To Come: A Study in Biblical Eschatology* (Grands Rapids, MI: zondervan Publishers 1965), 480.
44 George N. H. Peters, *The Theocratic Kingdom,* vol. 2 (Grand Rapids, MI: Kregel Academic & Professional, 1952), 129.
45 Acts 2:20.
46 Isaiah 4:2.
47 See Isaiah 24:23.
48 See Isaiah 35:2; 40:5; 60:1–3, 7.
49 Hebrews 12:1.
50 See Hebrews 12:1–2.
51 Ephesians 4:21.
52 John 8:12.
53 See Hebrews 12:2..
54 See John 5:30; 8:28, 42; 12:49.
55 See John 17:4.
56 2 Corinthians 3:18; Romans 8:28–29.
57 See Colossians 1:12.
58 See Ephesians 2:7.

SIX

MADE
TO RULE

*Our lives are a working out of the processes of creation.
All our ambitions and intelligence are beside that great elemental point.*

Saint Augustine

In the movie *The Lion King*, King Mufasa shows young Simba the whole kingdom of Pride Rock. After recounting the event later to his uncle Scar, young Simba says, "I'm gonna be king of Pride Rock...my dad just showed me the whole kingdom. And I'm gonna rule it all."

While this is just a movie, we can relate to young Simba's desire to rule. It is even more appropriate for us to have the same wonderful aspiration: *to rule it all.*

That's right, God created us to rule. Ruling is where glory to God finds its ultimate expression. Ruling done God's way is glory for Him because it expresses His attributes and the purpose for which He created us.

Looking back to the origin of everything that exists confirms the reason we were created—or for that matter, why everything was created: to be the realm of His rule and to be the rulers. God created everything to serve His kingdom purpose for the sake of His own glory. And He created the earth as the realm of our rule. We were created to rule that realm and bring Him glory in the process. Hear us roar!

CREATED FOR KINGDOM

God was not bored one day in eternity past and driven to create something for His pleasure by the monotony of it all. God has purpose in everything He does; doing something without purpose implies indifference or a lack of sufficiency. But God is completely content within Himself and is self-sufficient (all sufficient), so for Him to create assumes purpose. You and I are the pinnacle of His creation and He created us for purpose.

In the opening chapter of the Bible we learn that God created both man and woman in His own image; the likeness of the godhead.[1] Man was created to be unique among all the living creatures. That purpose becomes clear in the creative deliberation with the godhead where it says, "Let Us make man in Our image, according to Our likeness; and let them rule."[2] That purpose is confirmed two verses later:

> God blessed them; and God said to them, "Be fruitful and multiply, and fill the earth, and subdue it; and rule over the fish of the sea and over the birds of the sky and over every living thing that moves on the earth."[3]

This blessing was not like a toast at a wedding celebration, where the best man wishes blessings on the newly married couple. Here the Creator, sovereign over the universe, blesses to give direction and purpose to His creation and the creature made in His likeness. God said to "subdue and rule" everything.

The word translated "subdue" is the Hebrew word *kabash* and means to subjugate, bring in to bondage, dominate. The word "rule" is the Hebrew word *radah* and means to have dominion over. As Alva J. McClain explains, this term "was used later significantly of the reign of Messiah Himself in His kingdom: 'Rule in the midst of Your enemies' (Psalm 110:2)."[4]

Man was created for regal purpose.

The realm of the rule that God had for him was the whole earth, for "man is a king, and not a king without domain; the world around, with all the works of creative wisdom, is his kingdom."[5]

> *Man was created for regal purpose.*

Anyone who has ever purchased a home understands the high of a first-time home buyer. Nothing compares to the thrill of walking into your new home for the very first time. You signed all the papers, the keys are in your hand, and in you walk. It may be a man thing, home being a man's castle and all, but there is something special about being a new homeowner. You feel like a king!

The earth was created for man to rule, and man was created to rule the earth under the sovereign rule of God. In his book *Heaven*,

Randy Alcorn picks up on this very theme:

> God is the sovereign ruler of the universe, yet he
> chooses not to rule the universe alone.... God made
> human beings in his image, as creators and rulers, to
> carry out his divine will. He does not grudgingly pass
> on to us management responsibilities. On the contrary,
> he delights to entrust Earth's rule to us.[6]

God created man so that man would be the intermediary of His kingdom work on earth, a wonderful picture of true sovereignty. To this end the Father was delighted to pronounce that blessing of purpose upon man.

Rule!

KINGDOMS COLLIDE

Though it was Simba's right to rule over the kingdom his father had given him, he was tricked into losing it all by his wicked uncle. Scar's desire to be king led him and those who followed him to ultimate destruction. This storyline is nothing new under the sun.

Scene: Garden of Eden. Enter: the villain.

Seemingly out of nowhere comes a crafty snake with an array of devious ways to bolster his devilish plans. This evil snake in the grass deceives both Adam and Eve so that they unknowingly surrender their God-given position and authority to rule the earth.

It is from that point on in the pages of Scripture and history that we see two kingdoms in conflict.

The sudden appearance and existence of this evil one sheds further light on God's work in creation and purpose for the kingdom. God created the earth as the stage on which to play out His absolute dominion over the rebellious fallen angel and his kingdom of darkness.

Before the earth was created, much was taking place in the dimension of eternity past. Before time, there was a cosmic battle going on between good and evil.

In his commentary on the book of Matthew, pastor and author Stu Weber comments on this precipitating event:

> Let us step back and put this all together in basic terms. Somewhere in the far reaches of eternity past there was only God. In his own wisdom, according to his own counsel, he added the first forms of created intelligence—angels, magnificent inhabitants of the spirit world, myriads of them. We know that the most magnificent of all these creatures, the chief angel, was Lucifer, sometimes referred to as the Star of the Morning, or the Son of the Dawn. These angelic beings were part of the great timeless and boundless kingdom of God. We do not know a lot of details, but we do know the big picture. Many believe that the chief angel, the acting prime minister if you will, rebelled because of deep-seated pride: "Wickedness was found

in you" (Ezek. 28:12–19). This mighty celestial being became enamored with himself and infatuated with the concept of his becoming independent of Almighty God. He decided he would become "like the Most High" (Isaiah 14:12–15). Under his arrogant and usurping leadership, about a third of the angels rebelled against God (Revelation 12:1–9), forming a kingdom of their own, a counterfeit kingdom of darkness (Isaiah 14:12). This evil angel became, of course, God's chief adversary, the very meaning of the name Satan.[7]

The snake that pops up in this delightful Garden scene is none other than God's adversary, Satan. He is the slithery king of a kingdom that is contrary to God.

The war began before time and before the earth was, but it now had moved on to the main stage where man was created to play a vital role in its ultimate demise.

The battle is on.

KINGDOM CONFLICT

God's kingdom plan makes perfect sense against the backdrop of this larger-than-life cosmic battle that began before time. God's earthly kingdom, which began at Creation and will culminate in the second coming of the Messiah, was planned before the foundation of the world.[8]

Had man lived up to his original purpose he would have been

the ruling authority upon the earth still and to this day. The only condition for this to take place was for man to choose to commune with God and live a holy life. If man had met that condition it would have resulted in glory to God and victory over the kingdom of darkness.

Man was, however, created as a being with free will, and that free will came under serious temptation when the serpent twisted God's words and purpose and deceived Eve and then Adam. The consequences of that free choice were devastating. Man relinquished his dominion to Satan, who gladly usurped and assumed the role.

It is for this reason that the Bible calls this usurper the "god of this world."[9] This name certainly gives us some indication of his personal power. When Adam and Eve surrendered their reign, Satan became the god of this world and the whole world became the "domain of darkness."[10]

When Adam and Eve disobeyed God, they did not lose heaven or their eternal destiny; they did, however, surrender their kingdom on earth and their divinely appointed right to rule. By listening to Satan, they committed high treason and surrendered their regal authority.

Their sinful choice to obey Satan was not only personal to them; it became personal for all who would follow them.[11] As one author aptly puts it, "They who should have been deployed became employed by an evil taskmaster. The rulers became the ruled."[12]

As a result of the sin of our parents, Adam and Eve, every

generation to follow is born in sin and dead in trespasses and sin... by nature children of wrath...and alienated from the life of God.[13]

While Satan's dominion has a shelf life, God is allowing him a very pervasive role wherein the "whole world lies in the power of the evil one."[14] Satan is permitted to rule as the king of the air over those who are alienated from the life of God.[15]

The book of Job teaches us that this cosmic battle is taking place until this very day, because Satan is roaming the earth and seeking someone to devour.[16] Satan's kingdom of darkness is at work to blind the minds of the unbelieving[17] and rob God's children of the fellowship we can have with Him as we prepare for the coming kingdom.[18]

This cosmic kingdom conflict is the only reasonable explanation for why evil exists in this world. We live in a fallen world that is presently under the domain of the adversary of God.

Yet we are still left with probing questions. Stu Weber gets at the heart of this curiosity: "The question naturally arises, If God is sovereign, why did he let this happen? Why did he not just destroy the devil and his kingdom of darkness?"[19]

Weber's questions are ones most of us have asked. He goes on in his commentary to tell that it is God's plan to destroy Satan and his kingdom. And that this kingdom plan of God's has been set in motion to make His glory known in the most obvious and undeniable of ways. Crushing the ruler of this world, demolishing all that he has worked to build and all of its wickedness, will cause

God's holiness and righteousness to shine unlike ever before!

God knows best the way to glory Himself to the greatest degree.

The kingdom is it.

God created man for regal purposes to rule the earth. If man had continued to walk in fellowship with His creator instead of buying "hook, line, and sinker" into the lie of the adversary, he could have eliminated the existence of the kingdom of darkness. As a result of his own doing, man handed victory over to the usurper and that usurper gladly took control.

But the story is not over yet!

THE VICTORY IS CERTAIN: A KING PROMISED

In those early chapters of Genesis we find that as a result of the Fall, the theocratic kingdom was handed over to Satan. Yet God acted immediately by pronouncing a curse first on the crafty snake, the devil, and then the woman and finally the man.

The curse put upon man meant that nothing was going to come easily in his labor on earth.[20] For the woman, the curse was going to make what was originally intended to be a pleasurable experience painful.[21] This curse was also going to result in division and frustration between man and woman, for they would struggle at being a team.[22]

But in terms of the kingdom battle, a curse was put upon Satan that sealed his fate and the fate of his kingdom of darkness once and for all. The curse upon this snake is a promise of a king who would not fail in victory.

This is the first of many promises of a coming divine Messiah.[23] This curse upon Satan is a promise of another Adam that would come and take back the rule of God's kingdom.[24]

There is no question that the dark domain of Satan is temporary. God has a plan to defeat the kingdom of darkness once and for all. Upon contemplating the creation account, the psalmist David declared:

> O Lord, our Lord, how majestic is Your name in all the earth, who have displayed Your splendor above the heavens! From the mouth of infants and nursing babes You have established strength because of Your adversaries, to make the enemy and the revengeful cease. When I consider Your heavens, the work of Your fingers, the moon and the stars, which You have ordained; what is man that You take thought of him? And the son of man that You care for him? Yet You have made him a little lower than God, and You crown him with glory and majesty! You make him to rule over the works of Your hands; You have put all things under his feet, all sheep and oxen, and also the beasts of the field, the birds of the heavens and the fish of the sea, whatever passes through the paths of the seas. O Lord, our Lord, how majestic is Your name in all the earth![25]

David understood that man was originally created to rule, but the words of this song go far beyond God's original creation of Adam and Eve, for this is a song of praise with prophetic significance. The writer of Hebrews, over a thousand years later, applied these verses in reference to the promised Messiah, Jesus Christ, and the glorious future of His coming kingdom.[26]

The earth is the place where the cosmic battle becomes visible. God has promised that the earth is where this righteous kingdom plan will be resolved in His way and timing. God created the earth, and man, as a part of His plan to establish a kingdom that would ultimately bring the kingdom of darkness to an end. Despite our failings, God remains faithful to bring Satan's kingdom to its knees.

And to its knees it will come!

Paradise will be regained!

Today, neither man nor Jesus is ruling. While Satan's power suffered severe damage by Christ upon the cross,[27] the ultimate victory is yet to be realized. The final and consummate victory will be established in the coming kingdom of the promised seed.

Today Jesus is our High Priest, but He is not yet the king.[28] While there has always been some semblance of a universal rule of God, where God rules in our hearts by faith, this is a far cry from all that is intended and expected in the final outcome of the cosmic battle between God and Satan and the kingdom of darkness.

While Christ is head over all things to the church now, in the coming age He will have all things in submission to Him.[29] This kingdom victory is described for us in detail in Revelation 19. It is a dominant victory; that much is certain.

WHAT LIES AHEAD

Understanding the purpose of God in creation and the cosmic battle that rages behind the scenes should answer many of the probing questions we have. Why do bad things happen to good people? Why is there so much pain and suffering in the world? Why are people so evil and hurtful?

> *The answer to the kingdom of darkness is the kingdom of His beloved Son.*

The answer to these question and all others like them is that the kingdom of this world is a kingdom of darkness whose ruler is the adversary of God. There was a cosmic battle raging before the earth was. That battle gained a grip on this earth when sin entered and man relinquished his dominion authority.

That battle continues to this day, but it won't last forever.

The solution to the kingdom of darkness is "the kingdom of His beloved Son."[30] God has promised a kingdom on earth, and it is coming through the last Adam. It is through this victorious king that man has the privilege to gain back a share in the kingdom and rule with Christ.

The fallen angel who is temporarily the ruler of this world is the same one who tempted Jesus when he "took Him to a very high mountain and showed Him all the kingdoms of the world and their glory; and he said to Him, 'All these things I will give You, if You fall down and worship me.'"[31] Jesus did not fall for this trick, for He knew that all of it would be His in God's perfect timing.

Man has been created for kingdom and won't be satisfied until that kingdom is established. We have allowed our idea of heaven to replace the full creation purpose, but because we are created to rule for the glory of God, nothing less will truly satisfy.

UNTIL THAT TIME...

Satan blinds the minds of the unbelieving so that they do not come to a saving knowledge of God.[32] But even if the scales come off and we see the light of the grace of God, Satan does not stop there. If he is not successful in blinding us to the gospel of Christ, he robs our hearts of the kingdom message before it can take root and change our lives.[33] As long as he can steal this life changing message, he robs us of the joy that comes from sharing in the future possession of the kingdom.[34]

Our initial faith in Christ as Savior delivered us "from the domain of darkness and transferred us into the kingdom of His beloved Son."[35] It is through this deliverance that we are given a new assignment. Our faithfulness to Christ, however, is what determines our level of participation in the coming kingdom.

Satan will do everything he can to keep us from gaining that reward. Satan attacks now through the flaming missiles he relentlessly sends our way in the form of temptation. All of those temptations are to keep us from being faithful. We are reminded that our present battle is not with what we see (it is behind the scenes), but against this kingdom of darkness.[36]

But we have a means of shielding ourselves from those missiles of temptation; we armor up and fight.[37] At times it is appropriate for us to stand our ground with the devil.[38] Other times, however, when we are confronted with temptations in areas where we are particularly weak, the most appropriate thing for us to do is to run, so that we live to fight another day.[39]

We can win little battles because of how great Christ is in us through the Holy Spirit.[40] The war, however, won't be won until Jesus comes back to earth triumphantly to wage war.[41]

God began something at Creation, and despite the Fall, He will bring it to completion. That plan will be consummated on this earth, not in heaven. God will finish what He started here, before eternity!

We have been created for a purpose: to rule. You and I will not be satisfied with anything less.

In the future kingdom of Christ, we will have the opportunity to fulfill the purpose for which we were created: to bring glory to God as we rule with Christ.[42]

When young Simba lost his way and forgot his purpose, Mufasa came to him in a dream vision and said, "You have forgotten who you are and so forgotten me. Look inside yourself. You are more than what you have become. You must take your place in the circle of life." We have been created for a purpose and we must not forget who we are. We were created to rule and the promise to do so still remains.

We must take our place. It's our *Majestic Destiny!*

NOTES

1 See Genesis 1:26–28.
2 Genesis 1:26.
3 Genesis 1:28.
4 Alva J. McClain, *The* Greatness *of the Kingdom* (Winona Lake, IN: BMH Books, 2001), 43.
5 Franz Delitzsch, as quoted in McClain, *The Greatness of the Kingdom,* 43.
6 Randy Alcorn, *Heaven* (Carol Stream, IL: 2004), 203–4.
7 Weber, *Holman New Testament Commentary: Matthew,* 7.
8 Matthew 25:34.
9 2 Corinthians 4:4.
10 Colossians 1:13.
11 See Romans 5:12.
12 Myles Munroe, *Rediscovering the Kingdom* (Shippensburg, PA: Destiny Image Publishers, 2010), 56.
13 See Romans 5:12; Ephesians 2:1, 3; 4:18.
14 1 John 5:19.
15 See Ephesians 2:1–3; 4:18.
16 See Job 1:7; 1 Peter 5:8.
17 See 2 Corinthians 4:4.
18 See 1 John 2:28; 1 John 3:6-10 .
19 Weber, *Holman Commentary: Matthew,* 8.
20 See Genesis 3:17–19.
21 See Genesis 3:16.
22 See Genesis 3:16. The desire the woman would have for her husband was to usurp, and yet man would naturally rule over her in inappropriate ways.
23 See Genesis 3:15.
24 Ibid.
25 Psalm 8.
26 See Hebrews 2:6–8.
27 See John 12:31; 14:30; 16:11.
28 See Hebrews 3:1–6.
29 See Ephesians 1:21–22.
30 Colossians 1:13.
31 Matthew 4:8–9.
32 See 2 Corinthians 4:4–6.
33 See Matthew 13:4, 19.
34 See Matthew 25:21, 23.
35 See Colossians 1:13.
36 See Ephesians 6:12.
37 See Ephesians 6:11, 13.
38 See James 4:7.
39 See 1 Corinthians 6:18; 10:14; 1 Timothy 6:11; 2 Timothy 2:22.
40 See 1 John 4:4.
41 See Revelation 19:11.
42 See 2 Timothy 2:12.

SEVEN

BUILDING KINGDOM HOPE

The word which God has written on the brow of every man is Hope.

Victor Hugo

Imagine. Let your mind wander and imagine a whole new world.

God dwells visibly here. There is no sickness and no disease; no cancer, leukemia, strokes, heart attacks, not even a common cold. There is no heart-wrenching human tragedy or suffering. No more plane crashes, suicide bombings, starvation, homelessness, or child abandonment.

Instead, there is perfect peace and harmony. All the peoples of the earth speak one language and justice reigns absolutely. There is tranquility in every sense. The movements of nature have found their calm and rest within the sublime. All is beauty. All is provided. All is secure. All is as is it should be.

Can you see it in your mind?

Can you imagine?

We all long for such a utopia.

This imagined world may sound like a dream, but this dream world is actually the dream of the Father Himself. Unlike human dreams, which are more like wishes, this dream will come true on this earth in the culmination of history in the kingdom of Messiah (before eternity).

The world will be as one.

The images you saw in your mind portray only a few of the many promises God gave us in the Old Testament. On those promises, we build our perspective of the kingdom of Christ, which will take place here on earth before eternity: the millennial reign of Messiah.

In this chapter we will examine more closely the Scriptures that tell us about this coming kingdom and its King. You need to be sure of what they say so that your understanding has a solid foundation. So, roll up your sleeves and let's dive deep!

KINGDOM SURVEY

The Old Testament is the segment of the Bible which formulates our in-depth knowledge about the future kingdom of Messiah. But how many of us who have been in church much of our lives really understand that? How many of us even have a solid understanding of what the kingdom is?

In the world of pastors, missionaries, Christian authors and speakers, evangelists, and every day churchgoers, we often hear the phrases "Doin' it all for the kingdom" or "It's all kingdom work." But what in the world does that mean?

For some people, it means that they see the body of believers as the kingdom, and they are working to increase its size by bringing others into that kingdom, by leading them to Christ. They may also see the kingdom as the reigning of Christ in their hearts. There's nothing disastrously wrong with these thoughts, except that they are incomplete and not totally harmonious with the teaching of kingdom in the Bible.

For others, saying such things promotes the thought that if we work together as believers we can spur on the kingdom to be fulfilled. It's saying that our efforts of service and sacrifice will, in essence, create the peace on earth we all long for.

But none of these is what the Bible teaches us about the coming kingdom of Christ.

GOING DEEPER

Historically, there are three primary views on the topic of kingdom and dealing with the promises of the Old Testament. The latter two are most predominant.

Kingdom Realized. The kingdom as described will be realized through the preaching of the gospel by the church, not Christ's literal presence, and will be political, social, and spiritual.

Kingdom Now. The kingdom as described is the spiritual and universal rule of God n our hearts.

Kingdom Future. The kingdom as described will come to pass in the future in the earthly reign of the promised Messiah. The favored nation is Israel, and Christ will rule the earth on a literal throne of David from Jerusalem.

The most significant distinguishing difference between the two most predominant views (#2 & #3) is the method of interpretation. While both groups hold to a literal method of interpretation, when it comes to prophecy the Kingdom Now group adapts a spiritualizing method, or what is often called an allegorical method.

With this method the interpretation of prophecy becomes very subjective; some prophecies are taken literally while others are interpreted to fit the theological perspective of the interpreter. The literal method on the other hand interprets all of these prophecies literally. This is the preferred method because only by it is the meaning and intent of the original Biblical author maintained, producing the greatest harmony between the Old and New Testaments.

A CAUTIONARY WORD

God's adversary, the devil, does not want us to grasp the truth about the kingdom; this is because, as we saw in the last chapter, the kingdom of Messiah will be the greatest display of the glory of God and will bring utter destruction to his kingdom of darkness.

Satan goes so far as to steal the truth, or word, of the kingdom right out of our hearts before it can take root and produce fruit.[1]

So, arm yourself for battle and put on the full armor of God.[2]

THE KING TO COME

The earliest recorded promise of the coming King is found in Genesis 3, where we read that this King will be a member of the human race: "her seed."[3] This prophecy promises a singular seed, not seeds, so it is speaking about a specific One who is to bring victory over the serpent and his kingdom of darkness.

The promise of the seed of the woman is clarified later as one who would be a direct descendant of the patriarch Abraham.[4] Abraham had a son by the name of Isaac who had a son named Jacob, whose name was changed to Israel.[5] Jacob had twelve sons which become the twelve tribes of Israel/the nation of Israel.[6]

Of special note is the fact that the name Israel is never used in any other way throughout the Old Testament; it is used only for Jacob and the twelve tribes that develop from his twelve sons. The coming righteous ruler, the promised seed of the woman, would come through the tribe of one of those twelve sons: Judah.[7]

From the tribe of Judah arose a man named Jesse who had a number of sons, but David, his youngest, was given a promise that the prophesied seed of the woman and the King promised to Abraham would be his descendant. His kingdom, therefore, would never fail, and His rule on the Davidic throne over Israel would never come to an end.[8]

In the Prophets, we are told that this coming Davidic King would be born to a virgin.[9] And when that birth took place, it would be in a sleepy little town six miles outside of Jerusalem, called Bethlehem.[10] His father would have to be of David's line to qualify his son as heir to David's throne.[11] Though born in very humble circumstances, the baby was Jewish royalty.

It is starting to feel a lot like Christmas!

These prophecies were fulfilled in the person of Jesus from Nazareth in His first coming. Born to His mother Mary, a virgin, he was a "seed of the woman," a member of the human race, and related to Adam. Luke traces the genealogy of Jesus all the way back to Adam,[12] and Matthew traces His genealogy to Abraham, with emphasis on Jesus' relation to David.[13]

Do you see how the covenants God made to Abraham and David are tied to Jesus the Messiah?

Both of these covenants become the basis for the Messianic hope of Israel: they would one day have their own king, out of the line of David, ruling over them in the land God promised to give them as an eternal possession. No disobedience on the part of Israel would nullify these covenants, guaranteed by God.

In addition, even though Mary and Joseph lived nearly eighty miles away in Nazareth, Jesus' birth took place in the little town of Bethlehem.

What are the odds?

While many of these prophecies were fulfilled in the first coming of Messiah, many other prophecies remain unfulfilled. The unfulfilled prophecies speak to the nature of His reign—when the government will be upon His shoulders,[14] He will defeat the enemies of Israel,[15] and He will destroy the little horn of prophecy.[16]

These prophecies require His physical presence,[17] His immediate judgment over all the affairs between individuals and nations,[18] the reign of both His apostles over the twelve tribes of Israel[19] and His faithful servants who qualified for this rule,[20] and the end of all wars worldwide.[21] These prophecies and many more will be fulfilled in His second coming in triumph.

THE TIMING OF THE KING TO COME

As we read in the book of Hosea, the coming king and kingdom will only be after Israel experiences a long period "without king or prince, without sacrifice."[22] And the prophet Daniel, whose ministry took place in Babylon during the southern kingdom's exile, speaks on a number of occasions concerning a promised Messiah who would rescue and restore the nation of Israel back to the land after a long period of Gentile domination.[23]

Daniel's prophecy of the *seventy weeks* (seventy periods of seven equaling a period of 490 years) sets a chronological framework for that restoration of Israel for the fulfillment of the Messianic hope. It would be 483 years (sixty-nine weeks/periods of seven years), from the issuing of the decree by Artaxerxes in 444 BC to rebuild Jerusalem until "Messiah will be cut off and have nothing."[24]

The calculations have been done and the combination of those days (360 in a Jewish calendar year) was fulfilled precisely on the very day Jesus rode into Jerusalem on donkey to be rejected and eventually crucified. This would fulfill Daniel's prophecy of the Messiah being "cut-off."[25]

Daniel described the seventieth week as a period of great turmoil and destruction upon the nation and its prized city before the kingdom would be realized. While Daniel reveals some details of that seventieth week, the apostle John many years later receives detailed revelation about that period of seven years and records them in Revelation 6–18. This seven-year period of severe trials falling upon the earth is commonly called the Tribulation.

Jesus also spoke of this order of events and timing when he confirmed that the time of the kingdom's establishment would follow a great tribulation, the seventieth week of Daniel's prophecy.[26] After these weeks (periods of seven) are fulfilled, the Messiah will return to set up His kingdom.

That the timeline for the Messiah to return and reign immediately follows the terrible time of Tribulation is confirmed by the chronology of the book of Revelation.

McClain adds the following:

> The kingdom will not come "until" after a period of complete devastation in the land of Palestine (Isaiah 6:11–12; 32:13–18); until after a period of worldwide dispersion of the nation of Israel (Amos 9:8–10); until after a prolonged period when Israel will be "without king, and without a prince, and without sacrifice" (Hosea 3:4–5); until after a long succession of four world empires culminates in a world dictator whose terrible persecution will mark the end of Jewish suffering (Daniel 7:17–27); and until after a resurrection of godly Israelites (Daniel 12:1–3)."[27]

Nothing in known history of the world matches the events described.

The kingdom as promised is yet to be realized. Obviously!

HIS TRIUMPHANT COMING

While the promised first coming of Messiah was a royal presentation of the king and His fulfillment of the suffering servant,[28] His second coming will be triumphant and unmistakably cataclysmic.[29]

When the king comes in His kingdom—and He is certain to come, for the day is fixed[30]—it will be a coming that Daniel describes as a rock coming down from heaven smashing all the kingdoms of the earth (who are under the rule of the kingdom of darkness).[31]

The Bible gives us a clear picture of what will take place:

- Jesus will ride on a white horse, the kind of horse a leader rides into battle, and He will come to judge and wage war.[32]

- The name on His robe will tell it all: "KING OF KINGS, AND LORD OF LORDS."[33]

- He will remove all the wicked from the earth.[34]

- He will sit triumphantly on the "throne of David."[35] That throne is the same throne that Jesus calls "His glorious throne."[36]

The second coming of Messiah in triumph will be earth shattering.

- The government will be upon His shoulders[37] and there will be no limiting His rule or peace.[38] He will judge righteously in the land of Israel,[39] from Jerusalem.[40]

This second coming of Messiah in triumph will be earth shattering, and will bring an end to the times of the Gentiles.[41] These descriptions that apply to His second coming were not fulfilled in His first coming.

This much is certain.

STILL YET TO COME

Some promote the idea that we are now in the thousand-year reign of Christ, Satan is currently bound, and that Christ is ruling from His throne (in heaven).

Yet while Jesus *is* presently sitting at the right hand of the Father's throne, this should not be confused with the promises of His earthly rule and throne.[42] This role of Messiah as the rightful Davidic King is in the future, and is not the same as Christ's present ministry as our High Priest.[43]

George Peters, in his monumental work *The Theocratic Kingdom*, offers fifty-two reasons why the current ministry of Christ as High Priest cannot be equated with the coming rule of Christ on earth. All fifty-two reasons, based off the promises in the Old Testament, expect a literal fulfillment. As Charles C. Ryrie states,

> Because the King was rejected, the Messianic, Davidic kingdom was (from a human viewpoint) postponed. Though He never ceases to be King and, of course, is King today as always, Christ is never designated as King of the church.... Though Christ is a King today, He does not rule as King. This awaits His second coming. Then the Davidic kingdom will be realized (Matthew 25:31; Revelation 19:15; 20).[44]

And Walvoord agrees,

> The New Testament has fifty-nine references to David. It also has many references to the present session of Christ. A search of the New Testament reveals that *there is not one reference connecting the present session of Christ with the Davidic throne.*[45]

Regardless of any supposed similarities to our present experience, Christ is not ruling as king in fulfillment of the prophecies concerning the promised Davidic King who will rule over Israel in His future kingdom. When the Messiah King comes, the nation of Israel will be regathered back into the land of Israel,[46] and the Davidic King, the Son of Man, will be king over them.[47]

While Israel will be the favored nation of the kingdom,[48] all nations will benefit as was previously promised in God's covenant to Abraham and confirmed in the Prophets.[49] The connections to the guaranteed covenants God made with Abraham and David are unmistakable. In both of these covenants God guaranteed the irrevocable blessing of the Promised Land,[50] given to a particular people,[51] where all nations will be blessed,[52] for a divinely appointed, benevolent dictator to rule in all righteousness.[53]

There are also two additional covenants that will be fulfilled in this Messianic age. The first is the covenant of peace God guaranteed Israel so that they may live in the land securely and never be insulted again for the remainder of their existence.[54] And the other is called the New Covenant.[55]

Like so many topics in prophecy, this covenant has been

spiritualized to only be a reference to Christ's redemptive death for man's salvation; but this covenant is much more than that. The New Covenant was given to the nation of Israel, and in addition to dealing with the problem of committed sins, it will renew their hearts in such a way that personal righteousness will be guaranteed. This covenant, then, assures the spirituality of every saved man in the coming kingdom.

This will be unprecedented glory for God and for men to share.

The King and His kingdom will not fail.[56]

THE KINGDOM TO COME

Our present living conditions make it difficult to imagine living in a world where utopian conditions could exist, but that is the description of the coming kingdom. Our world is so full of social, religious, political, and economic deviation, turmoil, and chaos that it is nearly impossible to imagine the world God has planned.

The earthly Messianic kingdom will be populated by mortal bodied believers who are alive at the end of the Tribulation. These mortal bodied believers repopulate the earth during the reign of Christ.[57]

The kingdom of Messiah will bring a new social, political, economic, religious, and judicial environment. It will be utopia *ad infinitum*. Take a look:

JUSTICE:

The reign of Messiah will provide objective standards and moral absolutes which must be obeyed by these inhabitants of the earth.[58] He will rule by one set of spiritual and moral principles that are truthful, righteous, and just.[59] People will still make bad decisions and poor choices, but He will carry out justice of those absolute standards with a swiftness and immediacy we are not familiar with in our day.

In the kingdom, people will not stand in line to pay fines, get a lawyer, schedule a court date, or sit on a jury, because justice will be immediate.[60] When the King rules from His throne, anyone who has committed acts of wickedness will receive His loving, just discipline.[61]

The kingdom will bring social justice for all, and attention will be given to those areas of life that today tend to be ignored.[62]

How great is our need for the coming King like this?

RELIGION AND RULE:

His kingdom will be a kingdom of grace and salvation, the likes of which have never before been seen on earth.[63] While only believers survive the Tribulation and inhabit the kingdom in mortal bodies, the earth will be repopulated through natural procreation with humans who have the ability to freely choose to believe in Jesus Christ, who will be ruling in their midst. They will have all the revelation and ample opportunity.

The presence of nonbelievers who reject salvation, however, will not affect the political climate of the kingdom, because it is a righteous monarchy and the King will be the Messiah Jesus Christ, who will curb all unrighteousness by His righteous rule and immediate discipline. Jesus, the Messiah, will be an international authority for all people,[64] and He will rule from the worldwide central capital of Jerusalem.[65]

The King completely resolves the problem of religious freedom, for all will know that He is God and they will confess and bow down to Him.[66] There will be no more religious wars, or divisiveness, for there will be one religion, one world religious center,[67] and one center of worship.[68]

Since the King will also be a priest,[69] so there will, once again, be no separation of church and state.[70]

He will bring perfect harmony of religious and political/social life.

POLITICS AND MILITARY:

His kingdom will have no need of any branch of military, for the kingdom of darkness will suffer complete extinction upon the arrival of the King and His armies,[71] and Satan will be bound for the duration of the earthly kingdom.[72] There will be an absolute absence of war, and all militant expressions.[73]

People will dwell in peace and have nothing to fear.[74]

The kingdom will bring unprecedented global unity. People

will be able to communicate with one another regardless of origin or nationality, since all will speak a new pure language.[75]

The effects of these global changes will do wonders for the world economy!

NATURE:

All of life will be nurtured by the presence of the King and His rule.

The whole environment will be renewed.[76]

The animal kingdom will benefit: the lion will lie down with the lamb,[77] the bear will be a vegetarian,[78] little children will be snake charmers,[79] and nothing in the animal kingdom will do evil.[80]

Survival of the fittest will be no more.

The weather is going to be better as well. We will no longer need to build storm shelters, or purchase and install hurricane shutters, or preplan earthquake escape routes.[81] No more hurricane season, no longer a tornado alley.

The whole earth will see noticeable change in productivity, even the desert places.[82] Places of the earth today where a source of drinking water is scarce will be refreshed.

LIFE AND DEATH:

While those who inhabit the kingdom in mortal bodies will continue to experience natural life with birth, growth, and physical death,[83] life expectancy will return to pre-Flood possibilities. To die at one hundred will be understood as a life being cut short. Of course, the possibility of divine discipline is the exception.[84]

Life on this planet during the reign of Messiah will be qualitatively better than any time which precedes it. There will no longer be any sickness, deformity, or disease.[85] That is right. No need for emergency rooms, trauma centers, or even health insurance.

> ### *Life on this planet will be qualitatively better.*

The deep sadness a parent feels when they lose a child, or when a child is born without life, will be a distant memory.[86] Marriages will flourish, child neglect will cease, and the elderly will be tenderly cared for.[87]

The curse will be lifted and all of life will experience God's original design in paradise. It will be a phenomenal "glorification of nature."[88] This is what the creation is longing for.[89]

It will be glorious.

GOING DEEPER

Despite the graphic and clear nature with which these Old Testament promises speak about the kingdom, many have offered their own theological solutions, but "it is precisely at this point that most of the current views of the kingdom become woefully inadequate."[90] These are not descriptions of the eternal state because eternity is described in only the last two chapters of the Bible (Revelation 21–22) and will follow the earthly reign of Messiah upon this earth. And these vast and comprehensive Old Testament promises should not be spiritualized as if they are being fulfilled today, nor should they be misapplied to heaven or the eternal state. Dr. John Walvoord summarizes this point well:

By no theological alchemy should these and countless other references to earth as the sphere of Christ's millennial reign be spiritualized to become the equivalent of heaven, the eternal state, or the church as amillenarians have done. A righteous reign of Christ on earth is of course precisely what one would have expected from previous study of the Abrahamic covenant with its promises to the earth, the Davidic covenant relative to the Son of David reigning on the throne forever, and the many promises pertaining to Israel's regathering and reestablishment in their ancient land. The theocratic kingdom, therefore, of which the prophets spoke is an earthly kingdom which can find its fulfillment only in a literal reign of Christ upon the earth.[91]

PURA VIDA COMES UP SHORT

I grew up surfing the warm beautiful beaches of Southern California. For a child and young man, Southern California was as close to utopia as I could imagine.

Now I go back and can hardly handle the crowds. The beaches don't seem as warm or clean, and the whole environment seems to have changed for the worse. I have, however, on occasion found a few places that remind me of the feeling of my youthful utopian delight. I am very fond of Hawaii, but no matter how good the weather, the golf, or the waves. the cost of living prohibits Hawaii from filling my utopian void.

Costa Rica, on the other hand, is about as close as I can imagine to heaven on earth. The unofficial motto in Costa Rica is *pura vida*, meaning "pure life." The weather is great, the beaches are great, there is no shortage of golf courses, and when there are no waves you can drive ten minutes and be in a rain forest or at an active volcano. The food is delicious and did I mention the weather is great? As far as places on this planet go, Costa Rica is superb.

There are, however, problems with Costa Rica. The roads leave a lot to be desired, they speak a language I am not proficient in, and there is no military and seemingly very few police. I don't feel safe.

My closest utopia still doesn't quite do it for me. Nothing short of the kingdom of Messiah will do.

When He comes, it will be better than we can ever imagine.

His kingdom is the essential link in the chain of time and we must not overlook it. These promises give rise to kingdom hope!

NOTES

1 See Matthew 13:4, 19.
2 See Ephesians 6:11.
3 Genesis 3:15.
4 See Genesis 17:8.
5 See Genesis 35:9–10.
6 See Genesis 49:28; Exodus 1:7; 4:22.
7 See Genesis 49:10.
8 See Isaiah 11:1; Jeremiah 23:5; Isaiah 9:7; Jeremiah 33:15.
9 See Isaiah 7:14.
10 See Micah 5:2.
11 See Matthew 1:1–20.
12 See Luke 3:23–38.
13 See Matthew 1:1.
14 See Isaiah 9:6–7.
15 See Zechariah 12:9.
16 See Daniel 11:45.
17 See Matthew 25:31.
18 See Isaiah 2:4a; 11:1–5.
19 See Matthew 19:28.
20 See Luke 19:11–27.
21 See Isaiah 2:4b.
22 See Hosea 3:4.
23 See Daniel 2:31–45; 7:1–28; 9:24–27.
24 Daniel 9:26.
25 Luke 19:42.
26 See Matthew 24:29–30.
27 McClain, *The Greatness of the Kingdom,* 172.
28 See Isaiah 53.
29 See Daniel 2:????.
30 See Habakkuk 2:3.
31 See Daniel 2:44–45.
32 See Revelation 19:11, 15.
33 Revelation 19:16.
34 See Matthew 13:39–42, 49–50; 24:39–41; 25:32–46.
35 Isaiah 9:7.
36 Matthew 25:31.
37 Isaiah 9:6.
38 See Isaiah 9:7.
39 See Jeremiah 33:15.
40 See Isaiah 11:4, 9; Ezekiel 37:25.
41 See Luke 21:24; Romans 11:25.
42 Cf. Hebrews 1:3; 12:2; Revelation 3:21 with Matthew 19:28; 25:31.

43 Hebrews 2:17.

44 Charles C. Ryrie, *Basic Theology* (Wheaton, Ill.: Victor, 1986), 259.

45 Walvoord, *The Millennial Kingdom*, 203.

46 See Jeremiah 31:10; Zechariah 10:6; Ezekiel 37.

47 See Ezekiel 37:24; Matthew 25:31.

48 See Isaiah 11:121; Jeremiah 31:10; Micah 4:7–8; Ezekiel 36:11.

49 See Genesis 17:8; Isaiah 19:24–25.

50 See Genesis 13:14–17; 15:18; 17:7–8.

51 See Genesis 12:2; 13:16; 15:3–5.

52 See Genesis 12:2–3.

53 See 2 Sam 7:1–16; 23:1–5; 1 Chronicles 17:1–14; Isaiah 55:1–3; Psalm 89:20–37.

54 See Ezekiel 34:20–31.

55 See Jeremiah 31:31–34; Ezekiel 36:22–32.

56 See Isaiah 42:4.

57 See Isaiah 66:18, 20; Ezekiel 34:17–24; Daniel 7:22, 27; 12:1, 13; Matthew 13:38, 43, 49; 25:32–46 (Note: "eternal life" is a synonym for "kingdom" in the book of Matthew [cf. Matthew 19:16, 23–24, 28–30].)

58 See Isaiah 2:2; Zechariah 14:9; Psalm 72:8–11.

59 See Psalm 97:1–2; Jeremiah 23:5; Zechariah 8:3; Isaiah 59:14.

60 See Zechariah 14:17–19; Isaiah 66:24.

61 See Isaiah 40:4.

62 See Isaiah 40:10–11; 65:21–22; Amos 9:11, 14; Isaiah 61:4; Psalm 72:16.

63 See Joel 2:27–28; Zechariah 12:10; Psalm 84:11; Ezekiel 36:24–38.

64 See Isaiah 2:2, 4; Micah 4:3.

65 See Isaiah 2:3; Ezekiel 43:1–7; Psalm 110:2; Isaiah 60:10, 13, 17.

66 See Philippians 2:9–11.

67 See Isaiah 1:21; 2:3; 26; 60:14, 18; 62:3, 7; Zechariah 8:3; 14:16; Jeremiah 31:6.

68 See Zechariah 8:20–23; 14:16, 17; Isaiah 66:23; Malachi 1:11.

69 See Zechariah 6:12–13.

70 See Zechariah 14:7, 17–19.

71 See Revelation 19:11–21.

72 See Revelation 20:1–3.

73 See Psalm 46:9; Hosea 2:18; Isaiah 9:6–7; Micah 4:3–4.

74 See Micah 4:4.

75 See Zephaniah 3:9.

76 See Isaiah 65:17.

77 See Hosea 2:18; Ezekiel 34:25; Isaiah 11:6–8.

78 See Isaiah 11:7.

79 See Isaiah 11:8.

80 See Isaiah 65:25.

81 See Isaiah 2:19–21; 24:20; 30:23–26; Ezekiel 38:19–20; Zechariah 14:4, 8.

82 See Joel 2:21–24; Ezekiel 34:26.

83 See Isaiah 65:20
84 See Isaiah 65:20.
85 See Isaiah 33:24; 35:5–6.
86 See Ezekiel 47:12.
87 See Isaiah 42:3; Jeremiah 33:10–11, 15; Zechariah 8:4–5; Jeremiah 33:10–11; Zechariah 8:4–5.
88 Delitzsch, as quoted in McClain, *The Greatness of the Kingdom*, 235.
89 See Romans 8:19–22.
90 McClain, *The Greatness of the Kingdom*, 217.
91 Walvoord, *The Millennial Kingdom*, 298–9.

EIGHT

BORN
FOR KINGDOM

Life without a purpose is a languid, drifting thing.

Thomas à Kempis

In C. S. Lewis's *The Lion the Witch and the Wardrobe*, while the children are playing hide-and-seek, Lucy discovers a hidden door in the back of an old wardrobe. Through that door lies a new and wonderful world: Narnia.

Though Lucy enthusiastically tries to show the secret door to the other children, they see only the wardrobe—boxed in and confined, full of things one would expect to see in a closet. Their preconceived ideas about wardrobes keep their minds, at least at first, from seeing what lies beyond.

In similar fashion, many times our biblical assumptions and understandings function like that wardrobe. The wardrobe is the box of our own theology which we construct with solid walls and no doorways.

When those boxes are not big enough or are wrongly constructed, they keep us from something greater (even though we don't know something greater exists). And being theologically boxed in can be completely suffocating. If we linger too long, even when we finally realize there is a door, it may be all but too late to make much of an impact for the truth.

If, however, we can find an alternative door, it may lead us to a new world of understanding and insight. And when we break out of those poorly constructed boxes and walk through the door, we experience liberation and cry out, "Finally, I'm free indeed."[1]

Recently my barber, a good friend, was sharing with me the impact the teaching on the kingdom has had in his personal walk with Christ and his study of the Bible. He grew up in a Christian home, was a student of the Bible for years, and that interest deepened greatly as he grew older, got married, and had kids.

But for years he was frustrated in reading the Bible because so many passages seemed to contradict what he "knew" to be true. Since coming to understand the difference between heaven and the kingdom, he has been able to correct misunderstandings and reconcile difficult passages that in his previous reading he typically *skipped*.

He was boxed in and didn't even realize it...yet he certainly felt it.

With a biblical understanding of the kingdom, however, he not only found reasonable solutions to those frustrating passages, but he now feels liberated in his walk with God. Freedom is what the Son wants to provide for us, but we must abide in His Word, [2] not skip over it because it doesn't make sense to us or fit in our box.

As we turn to the New Testament with a firm foundation from the Old Testament, we should be prepared to break out of our "boxes" as we discover the hidden door that has been there all along. The New Testament teachings on the kingdom will help us unlock doors, uncover treasures, and offer new clarity that resolves difficult passages that we have struggled with for so long.

And most importantly, when we let Scripture speak for itself, its truth will set us free.

THE OLD AND NEW TESTAMENTS LINKED

We have a tendency to look at the Old Testament as good for Sunday school classes and lessons on humility and wisdom, and look at the New Testament as a sinner's guide to salvation and a Christian's guide to honorable social behavior. But the word of the Old Testament is the same as the New. Both point us to God's kingdom program for the earth: the coming kingdom of Christ.

The meaning of the term *kingdom* in the New Testament must be understood in light of the Old Testament unless we are given clear notification of changed meaning. Communication necessitates a common understanding of words, and if words or concepts change, it is absolutely natural to expect that some explanation of those changes be offered. With no further explanation or additional indication, the words would retain their original meaning. As Pentecost states,

> Truths related to the kingdom of God are not determined by the writings of men. Only through an inductive study of the Word of God may we understand this great subject. That means we must carefully study words according to their meaning to the original writers and readers; we must understand each passage according to its contexts (literary, historical, and cultural).[3]

This is essential to a literal interpretation of the Bible.

The Old Testament leaves off with burgeoning anticipation of a coming King and a kingdom. In the last book, Malachi, God promises to send His messenger, the Messiah, to purify the people, starting with the Levites, so that they will be spiritually ready to have the kingdom promises and covenants fulfilled to them.[4] God even promises to send the prophet Elijah to help in this spiritual revival.[5] This Elijah, as Jesus reveals to us later, is actually John the Baptizer.[6]

There is no missing link between Old and New Testaments: "Chronologically speaking, there is a four-hundred-year gap between Malachi and Matthew. Logically and thematically, however, there is no gap at all."[7] The life, ministry, and teachings of Jesus, and of those most closely associated with Him, show undeniably that the chain linking the Old and New Testaments is the earthly kingdom of Messiah.

Since God spoke so clearly through the prophets in the Old Testament, we should expect to see what He promised come to pass exactly in the way He said. The truth about the coming kingdom must be maintained in our reading of the New Testament, for it is essential to "preserve the integrity of the character of God."[8]

The kingdom is not just an old-time metaphor for something only prophets understood and cared about. It is truth. The kingdom is real. And it is coming.

With this understanding, the New Testament opens up like a blooming flower, first confirming Jesus' right to be the promised Messiah-King, and then quickly introducing John the Baptizer, whose job it was to introduce Jesus to the nation of Israel. The King had come and His forerunner, John, was preparing the way. They both offered the promised kingdom if the people would only repent and prepare themselves spiritually to be the recipients of it.

An old proverb says that if you chase two rabbits, you will catch neither. Often one rabbit is our presumptions, assumptions, or preconceived ideas, while the other is truth. If we are unwilling to suspend chase of our assumptions, the truth will certainly evade our grasp.

But if we are consistent as we chase the truth of the Kingdom, checking all things against the Scriptures, opening the door to a whole new world, we will obtain a freedom that is unimaginable. Consistency here will open up truths that have been previously hidden from us, or we did not know existed, because we were pursuing the wrong rabbit.

NEW TESTAMENT TALK OF THE KINGDOM

The New Testament opens with various announcements of the birth of Jesus, announcements brimming with Messianic kingdom hope. Alva J. McClain comments on the opening of the New Testament with a kingdom theme:

> *The New Testament opens brimming with kingdom hope.*

The New Testament period opens with several verbal announcements of a kingdom.... It was spoken of by angels: to Zacharias; to the virgin Mary; to Mary's husband, Joseph; and to the shepherds of Judea. It was anticipated by the Magi from the East. It was celebrated by the song of Elizabeth, by the Magnificat of Mary, and by the prophetic utterance of Zacharias.[9]

These birth announcements and their relationship to the kingdom must be understood in light of the historical context as spoken and understood by those who heard. When we read the New Testament today, we have a tendency to read it with a contemporary perspective from a post–New Testament worldview. This tends to prohibit us from understanding the intent of the original authors and recipients.

So in order to better comprehend what we are reading, we must don our first-century Jewish caps and think like they did.

Once we accept that the only biblical foundation these people had was the Old Testament, we will understand the sole basis of their worldview and outlook on life.

With respect to the Messianic kingdom, "It is a well-established fact that the Jews at the time of Christ were anticipating a literal fulfillment of the Old Testament theocratic kingdom promises."[10] This fact is true, irrespective of one's theology. As Peters commented,

> It has been universally admitted by writers of prominence...whatever their respective views concerning the kingdom itself, that the Jews, including the pious, held to a personal coming of the Messiah, the literal restoration of the Davidic throne and kingdom, the personal reign of Messiah on David's throne, the resultant exultation of Jerusalem and the Jewish nation, and the fulfillment of the millennial descriptions of that reign...they regarded the prophecies and covenanted promises as literal.[11]

For this reason we must interpret these announcements through this historical context.

Take, for example, the words of the angel Gabriel to Mary that the son to be born by her "will be great and will be called the Son of the Most High; and the Lord God will give Him the throne of His father David."[12] Keeping with the historical context, Walvoord asks, "How would Mary interpret such a prophecy? It should certainly be clear that Mary would consider this revelation a confirmation of the literal interpretation and literal fulfillment of the Davidic covenant"[13] which promises a king from the line of David to rule over the nation of Israel.

If that is what it meant to Mary, then that is what it meant!

To a Jew living in the fourth century BC (the year of Jesus' birth), *kingdom* meant the long-anticipated coming of Messiah and His literal earthly kingdom as promised. Neither Zacharias, the virgin Mary, Joseph, Elizabeth, the Magi, nor the shepherds would have spiritualized the truths being revealed as if they applied to some new form of spiritual kingdom, heaven, or eternity with God.

Jesus was born for kingdom—the literal earthly kingdom of Messiah.

A SALVATION UNTO THE KINGDOM

When Joseph finds out that Mary, his fiancé, is pregnant, he begins devising a plan to save both their names and reputations. But the angel of the Lord appears to Joseph in a dream and tells him not to be afraid and to continue to the wedding altar because the son that is to be born to Mary is of the Holy Spirit.[14] Then the angel makes a significant declaration: this son, who is to be named Jesus, "will save His people from their sins."[15]

The word *save* or *salvation* can have any number of meanings depending on its context, but the most common meaning in the Old Testament is "deliverance of His people from their struggles."[16] In many cases in the Old Testament, deliverance looks forward to the time of Messianic salvation, where God saves His people from their oppressors (which was a consequence of their sin) and sets up His kingdom.[17]

This use of the term *save* is not about salvation from the penalty for the sins one commits; it's about saving the nation from the consequence of their sins, which had led to oppression from their enemies and the absence of the glory of God. Joseph's understanding of salvation would have been based on the Old Testament and therefore been about the promised deliverance of His people into the kingdom of Messiah.[18]

The apostle Matthew makes the connection of the birth of Jesus to the Messianic kingdom by telling us that the birth was a fulfillment of the prophecy from God given through the prophet Isaiah:

> Now all this took place to fulfill what was spoken by the Lord through the prophet: "BEHOLD, THE VIRGIN SHALL BE WITH CHILD AND SHALL BEAR A SON, AND THEY SHALL CALL HIS NAME IMMANUEL," which translated means, "God with us."[19]

The historical context of the prophecy from Isaiah was directed to a sinful nation and is a promise of a coming King who would sit on the throne of His father David and reign over the house of Jacob.[20] The promised Messiah was to deliver the nation from their oppressors and restore what had previously been lost as they were reestablished in their own kingdom.

This idea of salvation as national deliverance was mentioned numerous times by the Old Testament prophets,[21] and would have naturally been the salvation every Jew was eagerly anticipating. And this is the full breadth of salvation Paul refers to in his letter to the Romans when he speaks about the future hope of Israel.[22]

In short, the salvation and kingdom heralded at the birth of

Jesus was to be for the deliverance of the nation and establishment of the kingdom of Messiah as expected from the Old Testament. After four-hundred years of silence, a child was born to bring salvation to the nation of Israel. Jesus was born to be their king.

CHRIST THE SAVIOR

Jesus was like any boy, but at the same time unlike any other boy. His focus on the things of God began early. In the NASB red-letter edition, the very first words that appear in red letters are from the lips of Jesus at age twelve. On this occasion a customary annual trip to Jerusalem had come to its natural end, but Jesus had different ideas than returning to Nazareth with His family.

After finally noticing His absence among the returning caravan to Nazareth, followed by a harried search of Jerusalem, Mary and Joseph find Jesus in the temple; He has been missing for three days. After being scolded for his anxiety-causing behavior, Jesus responds to their angst by asking why they are so concerned. He then proceeds to tell them the reason for his ill-perceived insubordination.

We can almost imagine the surprise, yet maybe even a bit of delight, when His parents hear: "Were you not knowing that I had to be in the things (literal reading) of My Father?"[23]

It is clear from the Old Testament that the Father's plan for the ages is the kingdom and that from an early age Jesus is interested in what interests the Father.

It is not difficult to imagine that Jesus was well aware of the many proclamations surrounding His birth. No doubt on more than one occasion growing up, when the whole family was around the dinner table, conversation involved those wonderful revelations and the supernatural circumstances of His birth. I would have loved to be a fly on the wall!

On this occasion Jesus said, "You should know why I stayed!" What a precocious (yet appropriate) start. A suitable start for the coming King who had been born with such phenomenal circumstance and promise.

The next time we hear from Jesus is some twenty years later, following his forty-day spiritual retreat in the wilderness.[24] He is in the synagogue of His hometown, and He is creating quite the stir. In the presence of many He reads a passage from an Old Testament prophet, promptly sits down, and tells everyone that the prophecy He read was fulfilled in their hearing that very day.[25] The quotation He read:

> THE SPIRIT OF THE LORD IS UPON ME, BECAUSE HE ANOINTED ME TO PREACH THE GOSPEL TO THE POOR. HE HAS SENT ME TO PROCLAIM RELEASE TO THE CAPTIVES, AND RECOVERY OF SIGHT TO THE BLIND, TO SET FREE THOSE WHO ARE OPPRESSED, TO PROCLAIM THE FAVORABLE YEAR OF THE LORD.[26]

That passage was a prophecy from the book of Isaiah, written seven hundred years earlier, describing for the nation of Israel their future deliverance when God would restore them to the land and establish Messiah's kingdom on Mount Zion. The "good news" that was to be proclaimed to a repentant and brokenhearted nation was that it was time for the kingdom. The imminence of the kingdom is the Good News that Messiah would preach to His people.[27]

The Good News fulfilled that very day: Messiah on the scene with *the gospel of the kingdom*. Now that is quite a unique gospel! It is not a gospel about how to get to heaven; it is a gospel about an earthly kingdom.

From His birth, into His adolescent years, and as He is ready to burst forth gloriously into His public ministry, Jesus is about one thing: the kingdom. Jesus was born with a purpose. He was born to be King. He was born for kingdom.

While we know in retrospect that the nation would reject Him and He would thus fulfill the promise of a Suffering Servant,[28] this in no way annuls His kingly right and destiny.

With this fuller understanding we should never celebrate Christmas the same!

Christmas is not about the hope of presents under the tree; it is about the burgeoning hope of the kingdom of Christ, the newborn king.

WHAT GOD IS ALL ABOUT

From the announcement of His birth all the way to His post-Resurrection appearances, the focus is emphatically upon the kingdom of Messiah. And Jesus' teachings have a clear and specific emphasis, and it is not heaven; it is the Messianic kingdom.

At no time did Jesus, nor any of the apostles, nor their disciples, use the term *kingdom* as a synonym for heaven, or for some alternative spiritual kingdom. The term *kingdom* is always a reference to the literal, earthly, Messianic kingdom as anticipated and expected from the Old Testament— that thousand years of Christ's reign on earth.

> *At no time did Jesus use the term kingdom as a synonym for heaven.*

As we look at the truth of the Scriptures as a whole, from the book of Genesis to the close of Revelation, we see that there is one main concept and one main theme. It was God's design to show us that the point of His entire plan, the reason He sent His son, was to open the doors to His coming kingdom even if the precursor was His death on the cross. Once we understand God's main thrust every passage we read has new meaning.

I hear the back of that wardrobe opening up to a new and wonderful world!

NOTES

1 See John 8:36.

2 John 8:31–32.

3 J. Dwight Pentecost, *Thy Kingdom Come: Tracing God's Kingdom Program and Covenant Promises Throughout History* (Grand Rapids, MI : Kregel Publications, 1995), 11.

4 See Malachi 3:1–4.

5 See Malachi 4:5–6.

6 See Matthew 17:10–13.

7 Pentecost, *Thy Kingdom Come,* 184.

8 Pentecost, *Things to Come,* 473.

9 McClain, *The Greatness of the Kingdom,* 268.

10 Pentecost, *Thy Kingdom Come,* 446.

11 Peters, *The Theocratic Kingdom,* vol. 1, 183.

12 Luke 1:32.

13 Walvoord, *The Millennial Kingdom,* 116.

14 See Matthew 1:17.

15 Matthew 1:21.

16 Joseph Dillow, *The Reign of the Servant Kings* (Haysville, NC: Schoettle Publishing Company, 1992), 113.

17 See Isaiah 12:3; 43:5; 45:17; Jeremiah 31:7.

18 To name just a few: Isaiah 33:22; 37:35; 63:1; Jeremiah 31:7; Zechariah 8:7; 9:16; 10:6.

19 Matthew 1:22–23.

20 See Luke 1:32–33.

21 See Isaiah 25:9; 33:22; 35:4; 37:35; 49:25; Jeremiah 2:27; 15:20–21; 30:10–11; 31:7; 36:29; Zechariah 8:7, 13; 9:16; 10:6.

22 See Romans 9:27; 10:9, 13; 11:26.

23 See Luke 2:41–51. The pluperfect tense used for the verb *know* in verse 49 implies that Jesus thought they should already have known this. The present infinitive of the verb ειμι (to be) indicates purpose: *I had to be to the things of My Father.* The word "house" (NASB) does not correspond to the original Greek word which is a neuter plural article (tois). The marginal reading in the NASB is closer: affairs (lit. "in *the things* of My Father".

24 See Luke 4:1–12. Jesus was led by the Spirit to be tempted by the devil.

25 See Luke 4:21.

26 Luke 4:18–19 (from Isaiah 61:1–2).

27 See Isaiah 60:1–22; 61:1–2.

28 Isaiah 53.

NINE

KINGDOM WITHIN GRASP

Like apples of gold in setting of silver is a word spoken in right circumstances.

Proverbs 25:11

Have you ever felt like the "village idiot"? You know, completely confused when it seems like everyone else around you gets it? Or thought you understood something, acted on your understanding, and then realized you had it all wrong?

A friend of mine told me a story of when she was in college training to become a teacher. One of her classes involved creating lesson plans and presenting them to the class. At this time in her life, she was engaged to be married and much of her time was spent planning her wedding and thinking of what her new life would soon be like.

It was her turn to give a presentation to the class. She stood up, brought all of her props to the front, and taught her lesson. All seemed to be going well, though some of her classmates looked a bit confused. After she concluded her lesson she sat down, feeling confident about her performance, and waited for class to end. Her professor stopped her on the way out.

"Now dear," she said, "I know that you are getting married soon and you may be a bit distracted."

"Um, yes?"

"Well, I'm sorry to tell you this, but the presentation you did was completely wrong. You didn't follow the guidelines at all. I'm going to have to ask you to redo it."

Ugh. What my friend had missed was crucial information. Yes, she was to give a presentation that day, and yes, she performed quite well, but she had totally missed the point of the assignment and was left feeling embarrassed and humiliated, with all of her work being for naught.

When we look at the Christian life, the Christian message, and what the Bible is speaking to us about, we don't want to miss that crucial piece of information, that piece of understanding that points us in the right direction. And therein lies a warning, for Satan would love nothing better than to have God's children working and striving, yet missing the mark.

How great it would be for the adversary of God to know he had deceived some of the saved into believing a lie—how delighted he would be to see the glory of God muted and diminished!

And even though the main message of the Bible is the coming kingdom of Christ, many of us have missed it; we've missed that crucial piece of information. We have been distracted by things, often things that are good, but haven't seen the bigger picture.

My desire, my goal, my heart is to help you look at the Bible, even those *problem* passages, and see how it all makes sense when we don't miss that crucial piece of information.

THE KING IS COME

It is often said you can't judge a book by its cover.

Appearance may misrepresent what is inside.

Jesus was born to be a King over a kingdom. He certainly didn't look like a king; He looked like a carpenter's son from the poor side of town. But His message was the offer of a kingdom, and only a king had authority to do that. And He never veered from this purpose.[1]

To understand Jesus' message we need to open the Book and look inside. The cover, we will find, actually veiled the glory of a King over all other kings, and yet His message will clearly reveal His purpose in coming: to fill the long vacant throne of David His forefather.

> *Jesus was born to be a King over a kingdom.*

But before we look to Jesus, let's look at the one who had the responsibility for paving the way for Him: His cousin, John the Baptizer.

Prior to John's birth, an angel of the Lord appeared to Zacharias, John's father, and promised that Elizabeth, his wife, would bear a son who would "turn many of the sons of Israel back to the Lord their God"[2] and would "go as a forerunner before Him in the spirit and power of Elijah."[3]

John's job was to initiate a spiritual revival, turning the hearts of "the disobedient to the attitude of the righteous so as to make ready a people prepared for the Lord."[4]

The Messianic implication is explicit. John was the forerunner of the long awaited Davidic King who would also be Israel's promised Messiah.

When John began his ministry, he preached a message that served as a warning to the nation of Israel. They needed to change their minds concerning the sins that were separating them from the blessings of their God. This change of mind (or heart) had to be followed up by actions consistent with their new mind-set.

The message of John was an urgent plea because the kingdom of heaven was at hand; it was eminent; it was coming. And the establishment of that kingdom required such a response.[5] On John's ministry, J. Dwight Pentecost comments:

> John as an Old Testament prophet proclaimed the same kingdom as the prophets. John announced a literal kingdom on the earth under the personal rule of God's covenanted Messiah. The establishment of this kingdom would fulfill the covenant God made with David, which promised that one of David's sons would

sit on David's throne and rule over David's house. John said this kingdom was near. Such a glorious promise was an impetus to bring the nation to repentance, and John's announcement generated widespread interest. Mark recorded, "The whole Judean countryside and all the people of Jerusalem went out to him."[6]

The message of John bears striking similarity to the message of the Old Testament, for there is "perfect, logical, literal, historical continuity among all of God's prophets."[7] Why should anyone expect it to be any different?

In like manner, when Jesus began His public ministry His message was the same in content and urgency as His cousin's: "Repent, for the kingdom of heaven is at hand."[8] That message is described a few verses later as "the gospel of the kingdom."[9]

Since we do not have any further explanation or clarification of the term *kingdom*, we must assume, as did those who heard the message themselves, that the kingdom being proclaimed by both John and Jesus is the same kingdom promised in the Old Testament.

The king was present, and He had authority to set up that kingdom if they would get their lives right. That is good news for the Jewish people, and the content of Jesus' main gospel message recorded in the Synoptic Gospels (i.e., Matthew, Mark, and Luke)!

This gospel had nothing to do with becoming justified before God; it did not promise anyone heaven as an assured destiny; it was not about being saved from hell.

A few things about this gospel message need to be clarified. We must understand:

(1) the term *gospel.*

(2) the terms and concept of the *kingdom of heaven.*

(3) the condition attached to entering this kingdom..

Understanding these three elements will help us maintain the biblical distinction between heaven and the kingdom of heaven and between the different conditions for gaining entrance into them.

So, here is more of that crucial information to keep us from missing the big picture.

GOSPEL

If someone were to ask what the gospel means, most Christians today would say, "It's that Christ died for our sins according to the Scriptures, and that He was buried, and that He was raised on the third day according to the Scriptures."[10] While this is an accurate description of current-day focus and usage, even with minor variation from person to person, it does not explain the term as used by Jesus in His preaching.

> *Jesus' gospel was not about salvation from sin's penalty.*

Jesus' gospel was not about salvation from sin's penalty or being justified. Consequently, it was not about His death, burial, and resurrection.

Don't miss this. The gospel of Jesus was about the promised Davidic kingdom for a specific nation chosen to serve Him in impacting and being a light to the rest of the world. *Jesus was not telling people how to get to heaven.* He was telling them what they needed to do for God to establish the kingdom He had promised them.

In the original Greek language of the New Testament, the word *gospel*[11] simply means *Good News*. The meaning or content of the Good News depends on the context: "A survey of the New Testament usage helps clarify the various nuances of the word, and one quickly concludes that the term gospel is not a technical term... the specific good news differs from context to context."[12]

In Jesus' preaching recorded in the Synoptic Gospels, the Good News is about this kingdom. So, if Jesus preached about it, it reveals what He is about. We need to try to understand everything we can about that which was so important to Him: the kingdom of heaven.

KINGDOM OF HEAVEN

The content of the gospel that both John and Jesus proclaimed was "the kingdom of heaven." Once again we are reminded that "the background of the New Testament idea of the Kingdom must be found in the Old Testament,"[13] and not in the theologies of the sixteenth and seventeenth centuries where the whole idea of a spiritual kingdom was proliferated.

It is for this reason that we must insist that the kingdom is the promised kingdom from the Old Testament. The propriety of this approach was long ago established by Peters for Christian interpreters when he said,

> John the Baptist, Jesus, and the disciples, employed the phrases "kingdom of heaven," "kingdom of God," etc., in accordance with the usage of the Jews...to designate a certain and definite Kingdom, and use it without the slightest intimation or explanation of a change in its meaning.[14]

Given that the term *heaven* modifies the term *kingdom*, we must seek to understand what that modifier tells us about the kingdom.

In the New Testament the term *kingdom* is modified in various ways: the kingdom of Christ,[15] kingdom of God,[16] the kingdom of His beloved Son,[17] and [Jesus calls it] His kingdom.[18] In one story, both *God* and *heaven* modify *kingdom* and are used interchangeably as synonyms.[19] Henry Virkler comments on this very issue:

> Several parallel passages within the Synoptics use the term "kingdom of God" when referring to a particular incident and the term "kingdom of heaven" when referring to a very similar incident mentioned in one of the other Gospels.... If these two are actually separate kingdoms, then Jesus would have been ascribing two entirely different meanings to highly similar parables told on separate occasions.... For these and other reasons the majority of evangelical expositors have understood these terms as synonyms.[20]

Heaven does not describe the location where the kingdom will be experienced, but rather its origination and quality. It is a kingdom that will come to earth and be experienced on this earth.

It will not only be *from* heaven, but it will manifest the same rule of God as is being exercised *in* heaven at this present hour.

It ought to be painfully obvious that neither God nor Jesus is ruling over the earth in the sense of having His righteous will carried out in all respects. This world is a mess; if this is the result of God's righteous rule, who would want more of it? The kingdom of heaven, then, is not a kingdom that takes place in heaven,[21] but rather one that has its quality because it comes from heaven, as did Jesus: at His trial at the end of His life, Jesus is asked whether He is the king of the Jews. He replies affirmatively and then adds that His kingdom is "not of this world...not of this realm."[22] McClain comments on this verse:

> "My kingdom not of this world"...the preposition is *ek*, indicating source or originating cause. His kingdom does not originate in the present cosmos or world system.[23]

While Jesus said that His kingdom does not originate from this world, He did not say it would not take place on this earth. In the same way that Jesus said His kingdom is not of this world, He also said, "I am not of this world."[24] This statement certainly refers to His divine origin and essence, not His locale. He was born on earth, and was standing on this earth when He made that statement.

When Jesus was enticed by the devil in the last of the three great temptations, He was offered "all the kingdoms of the world." Why would Satan offer this to Jesus? Why was this a real temptation? He offered it to Jesus because Satan knew why He had come.

He knew Jesus had come to fulfill the Old Testament prophecies and covenants concerning Israel's promised earthly kingdom. While Israel's kingdom would have its own territory, called the *Promised Land* in Scripture, her king would rule over the whole world and not just her kingdom.

Satan was offering Jesus what He came for, the kingdoms of the whole world, without a struggle, hoping that he might detour Him from the cross. In short, Satan was offering Jesus the crown without the cross, victory without a struggle. Satan knew that Jesus was born to be the King of kings and the Lord of lords. And he knew that His reign was predicted to be accomplished upon this earth through His physical presence here.

Furthermore, "the kingdom is characterized as the kingdom of heaven because it is patterned after heaven and its perfection."[25] A comment in the *Bible Knowledge Commentary* is helpful on this point:

> This rule was to be heaven's rule: "the kingdom of heaven." Does that mean God would then begin to rule in heavenly spheres? Obviously not, for God has always ruled over heavenly spheres since Creation.... God's heavenly rule was about to be extended directly to earthly spheres. God's rule over the earth had drawn near and was about to be instituted through the person of the Messiah.[26]

Also, when the prophet Daniel describes this coming kingdom, he does so with descriptions which are truly heavenly! Daniel said that the kingdom will be given to a king who comes "with the clouds of heaven."[27] It will come down from heaven like a rock which was "cut out without hands."[28] The dominion is given to the Son of Man by the "Ancient of Days."[29] And it is a kingdom which will not fail or be destroyed.[30]

The kingdom being proclaimed by Jesus is the same kingdom of a heavenly origination; it is divine in nature and not of this world, although it will take place on this planet. The kingdom of heaven is not heaven, nor a rule in heaven. Since Jesus gives no explanation of the kingdom He was offering, it must be because He knew quite well that those to whom He was delivering this gospel were well aware what the expected kingdom was.

So what's the big deal?

Why does it matter?

Is this really *crucial* information?

Absolutely. It reveals what God is all about. To mistakenly marginalize the kingdom here, and make it mean something like heaven or a spiritual kingdom, puts us in the limelight as the ones needing to be saved so we can go to heaven and removes God from center stage in the leading role He plays in the kingdom program on earth to crush the rebellion of Satan.

And if we make the assumption that the kingdom being proclaimed is heaven, it will be impossible to harmonize with the rest of the New Testament (even though some think they have done this).

Not only will some passages have to be spiritualized in order to explain them, but other passages will have to be massaged to make them appear to harmonize with basic tenets of the Christian faith. The latter includes things like justification by grace alone through faith alone, in Christ alone apart from any work.

The kingdom that Jesus and John preached necessitates repentance and good works, and cannot, therefore, be synonymous with the free gift of eternal salvation.

Understanding the big picture means understanding that the King has come, that He came to establish His kingdom, and that in His message He gave the conditions for those who would participate in that kingdom. Each piece of this picture is crucial information.

THE CONDITION FOR KINGDOM

The Old Testament prophets repeatedly declared that repentance was the condition that must be met by the nation of Israel for the kingdom to be realized. The nation had to "walk in the light,"[31] have "regard for [their] Maker,"[32] loathe themselves in their own sight because of the evil they committed,[33] and call upon the name of the Lord for God to answer and save them.[34] As the prophet Jeremiah so plainly states,

> "For I know the plans that I have for you," declares the LORD, "plans for welfare and not for calamity to give you a future and a hope. Then you will call upon Me and come and pray to Me, and I will listen to you. You will seek Me and find Me when you search for Me

with all your heart. I will be found by you," declares
the LORD, "and I will restore your fortunes and will
gather you from all the nations and from all the places
where I have driven you," declares the LORD, "and I
will bring you back to the place from where I sent you
into exile."[35]

God has a plan to prosper Israel, but Israel needs to repent and
turn to Jesus before God will execute His plan.

According to the Old Testament, the future restoration of
Israel will come only after their national discipline leads to "the
nation's repentance."[36] The reason the nation was without Messiah's
kingdom was that they remained in their disbelief and disobedience.
Naturally, the condition for the kingdom to be realized as promised
was that the nation return to God and become a righteous people.

It is no surprise, then, that both John and Jesus preached
the same gospel of the kingdom, and that both attach the same
condition for its reception and establishment. The word *repent*
simply means to "have a change of mind." This change of mind
is expected to result in a change of behavior; in fact, it ought to
have that effect. Nevertheless, the change in behavior is something
different from the required change of mind-set. This is the reason
that deeds worthy of repentance are commanded in the Scriptures
and not assumed to be part of the repentance itself.[37]

All of this was good news because the kingdom was "at hand."[38]
For the kingdom to be *at hand* "meant that the only thing preventing
the institution of the kingdom announced...was the repentance

of the nation."[39] The imminent possibility of a kingdom was true because of the identity and authority of the Person making the offer. Both John and Jesus could rightly say that the kingdom was at hand because it could happen without any precipitating events other than the condition prescribed.

The kingdom of God had come upon men through the presence of the King, His offer, and the King's demonstration of power to cast out demons and perform miraculous signs.[40]

The kingdom was near.

That was good news!

That was the gospel!

But they missed Him and so they missed the kingdom, for now.

Jesus' emphasis on the kingdom continued all the way to the cross and beyond.

For forty days after the resurrection He appeared to many, and the main subject that He taught His disciples remained the kingdom.[41] There was no mistaking His content; there was no confusion in the minds of the disciples on the nature of kingdom that He discussed with them; nothing had changed in His purpose or in His message.

There is not even a hint on the pages of Scripture that those who listened intently to Jesus thought He was talking about a "spiritual kingdom." They already had that kind of relationship with God anyway. That didn't need to come; it was already present. Those that heard the very words of Jesus for forty days understood full well that He was explaining to them the literal, physical kingdom that was promised in the Old Testament. Consequently, they only inquired about the *timing* of the kingdom's establishment. While He was not willing to satisfy their curiosity about the timing the kingdom would begin,[42] its coming was certain.[43]

In His first coming, Jesus Christ, the second person of the Trinity, was here to tender a genuine offer of the promised kingdom to Israel if they would at last repent. All of the messages by the angels, John the Baptist, Jesus, the Twelve, and the seventy were genuine offers of the earthly Messianic Kingdom. There is *nothing* within these offers of the kingdom of some subtle and disguised offer of heaven, salvation from sin's penalty, or eternity with God. Those ideas must be read into the text.

All these messages, united in content and purpose, offered what had been promised by God and expected by God's people. In the Synoptics, the gospel is about the kingdom of heaven, a kingdom of heavenly origin, but with an earthly future. The kingdom is conditioned upon repentance, good works, and proven character. Entrance is not based upon the free gift of eternal salvation (although it is certainly a prerequisite, see John 3:3, 5). Since the message about the kingdom requires more than faith from the believer, it cannot be about justification, or going to heaven; and it is a message consistently given to believers, not to the lost.

On the other hand, justification/salvation is always a free gift on the basis of *grace alone* through the instrument of *faith alone* (not works) in Christ Jesus.[44] Confusing these two issues will only lead down a gruesome path of legalism, fear, angst, and condemnation, accompanied by a lack of assurance. That is not good for anyone!

You must know that you are secure in God's love before you can live for Him and His glory.

From the opening pages of the New Testament the big idea, the main topic, is the kingdom and how to realize your full inheritance in it when you enter; it is not about how to get to heaven or how to be saved from hell. Jesus' message and interest were about the kingdom.

There is no new plan...no change of plans. Our confidence is bolstered knowing that God is the "same yesterday and today and forever."[45] He is consistent and can be counted on. To Him be the glory!

AND US?

It's ironic to me that the Jews couldn't see Jesus for who He was. It was as though they had been blinded to the truth. And yet the kingdom was something that was real to them, which they counted on and longed for. This fact remains true to this day. But they thought they deserved it on the basis of their genealogy alone. They missed it because of arrogance.

And we, we see Jesus. We love Him and have complete

confidence that He is our Savior. But many of us have been blinded to the kingdom and the significance of it to the Father and our own lives.

Satan doesn't have any new tricks, does he?

When we lack that crucial piece of information, we miss the point of the whole thing. My friend didn't fail that college class; she even made a 4.0 that year and became a teacher. But all of the efforts she had put into her presentation resulted in nothing in respect to her grade. If we miss the point which runs through the entire Bible, then we won't see the big picture.

It's not an issue of our eternal salvation; we will still enjoy eternity with the Lord as believers in Christ. But if we don't understand how our efforts done in faith and done for the glory of God will result in our participation in the coming kingdom, then we might lose heart and become discouraged. We might grow weary and faint. We might give up and have no will to persevere.

But once again, we can look to Jesus as the one who blazed the trail before us. We can look to Him, the one who was rejected, as to how we are to persevere.

NOTES

1 Mark 1:14–15, 38–39.
2 Luke 1:16
3 Luke 1:17.
4 Luke 1:16–17.
5 Matthew 3:1–2.
6 Pentecost, *Thy Kingdom Come*, 194.
7 Ibid., 180.
8 Matthew 4:17.
9 Matthew 4:23.
10 See 1 Corinthians 15:3–4.
11 The Greek term is euaggelion ("euangelion"), which is a compound word of eu ("good") + angelia ("message"). Thus the meaning of the word is "good message" or "good news." The context will determine the content of the news that makes it good!
12 J. B. Hixson, *Getting the Gospel Wrong* (n.p.: Xulon Press, 2008), 79.
13 McClain, *The Greatness of the Kingdom*, 19.
14 Peters, *The Theocratic Kingdom*, vol. 1, 195.
15 See Ephesians 5:5.
16 See Matthew 12:28. (Too many other references to mention.)
17 See Colossians 1:13.
18 See Matthew 16:28.
19 Matthew 19:23–24.
20 Henry Virkler, *Hermeneutics: Principles and Processes of Biblical Interpretation* (Ada, MI: Baker Academic, 2007), 168.
21 See Matthew 6:10.
22 John 18:36.
23 McClain, *The Greatness of the Kingdom*, 381.
24 John 8:23.
25 Charles L. Feinberg, *Premillennialism or Amillennialism*, as quoted in Pentecost, *Things to Come*, 434.
26 Walvoord, *The Bible Knowledge Commentary: An Exposition of the Scriptures* (Wheaton, IL: Victor Books, 1983–1985), S. 2:24.
27 Daniel 7:13–14.
28 Daniel 2:34.
29 Daniel 7:13–14.
30 See Daniel 2:44; 7:14.
31 Isaiah 2:5.
32 Isaiah 17:7.
33 See Ezekiel 20:43; 36:31.
34 See Zechariah 13:9; Joel 2:32; Romans 10:9–13.
35 Jeremiah 29:11–14.
36 Pentecost, *Thy Kingdom Come*, 168.

37 See Luke 3:4–6 (quoting Isaiah 40:3–5); Luke 3:10–11.

38 Matthew 3:2; 4:17. ἐγγίζω (engizō): vb.; 1. come near, draw near, approach, spatially; 2. come near, have a time approach. James Swanson, *Dictionary of Biblical Languages with Semantic Domains: Greek (New Testament)*. electronic ed. (Oak Harbor: Logos Research Systems, Inc., 1997), S. DBLG 1581, #2.

39 Pentecost, *Thy Kingdom Come*, 195.

40 See Luke 11:20.

41 See Acts 1:3.

42 See Acts 1:6.

43 See Acts 1:7. The time is "fixed"!

44 See Romans 3:27–29; Ephesians 2:8–9.

45 Hebrews 13:8.

TEN

THE NARROW GATE

I do not believe there is a problem in...the world today which could not be settled if approached through the teaching of the Sermon on the Mount.

Harry S. Truman

Oskar Schindler: I could have got more out. I could have got more. I don't know. If I'd just... I could have got more.

Itzhak Stern: Oskar, there are eleven hundred people who are alive because of you. Look at them.

Oskar Schindler: If I'd made more money... I threw away so much money. You have no idea. If I'd just...

Itzhak Stern: There will be generations because of what you did.

Oskar Schindler: I didn't do enough!

Itzhak Stern: You did so much.

Oskar Schindler [*looks at his car*]: This car. Goeth would have bought this car. Why did I keep the car? Ten people right there. Ten people. Ten more people.

[*Removes Nazi pin from lapel*]

Oskar Schindler: This pin. Two people. This is gold. Two more people. He would have given me two for it, at least one. One more person. A person, Stern. For this.

[*Sobbing*]

Oskar Schindler: I could have gotten one more person...and I didn't! And I...I didn't!

Those are the words of Oskar Schindler in the movie *Schindler's List* upon realizing the enormous gain that could have been accomplished through simple sacrifice. Oskar is pummeled by the full realization that something as inconsequential as a gold lapel pin or a car could save a human life, or two, or more; and that forfeiting something of little or no lasting value could lead to valuable gain.

Sometimes the greatest gain comes from the seemingly smallest of sacrifices or loneliest and narrowest of paths.

Hindsight provides opportunity for great wisdom, but also great regret.

Foresight, on the other hand...it is what Jesus offers in the Sermon on the Mount. This He did so there would be no regrets and so all could walk through the narrow gate to find fulfillment in this life and the age to come.

To waste opportunities is to have regrets, but to waste a life is a whole other story. To *not* walk through the narrow gate is to waste a life and forfeit your inheritance in the coming kingdom.

THE WAY TO LIFE

Jesus commanded His disciples and us, by way of application, to "enter through the narrow gate; for the gate is wide and the way is broad that leads to destruction, and there are many who enter through it."[1]

> *To not walk through the narrow gate is to waste a life.*

Half of that statement seems pretty scary, but what is Jesus saying?

The word *destruction* is a word that means "the destruction that one causes, waste; or the destruction one experiences, ruin."[2] The word does not mean hell! The only other time Matthew uses this word is in chapter 26, where the woman pours costly perfume upon the head of Jesus: "But the disciples were indignant when they saw this and said, 'Why this *waste*?'"[3]

This is a classic example where we must stop thinking in terms of our old "heaven and hell dichotomy" for this is not talking about eternal destruction, nor is the Sermon on the Mount about how to get to heaven. The broad way that leads to destruction is the avenue of a wasted life; a life that will be full of regrets...a life which has not earned the inheritance in the kingdom. Sadly, Jesus said "many are those who enter by [the broad way]."[4]

The flipside is when Jesus said that "the gate is small and the way is narrow that leads to life, and there are few who find it."[5] The small gate and the narrow way is nothing more than the content of the sermon He just delivered (Matthew 5–7). The result for one who lives this way is a full, rich and meaningful life that leads to greatness in the kingdom.[6]

The Sermon on the Mount is the explanation of the "gospel of the kingdom" which both John and Jesus were proclaiming.[7]

So in a way, this sermon is the "road map" to greatness in the kingdom.

EXPLAINED OR EXPLAINED AWAY

The Sermon on the Mount is one of the greatest motivational sermons ever delivered and the longest recorded sermon of Jesus. More than likely He gave it on more than one occasion.[8] If we pay close attention to what Jesus was actually saying in this sermon, it should inspire us to live for the kingdom.

Historically, however, this sermon has been seriously misunderstood and the powerful and motivating truth is missed and even perverted, causing harm. I can only imagine how Satan glories in that!

What a *dis*grace.

The interpretations of the Sermon on the Mount generally fall into two categories. Either the sermon is *explained,* or it is *explained away*.

Those who attempt to *explain it away* do so by indicating

that the practical teachings have no relevance for the church or the believer in Christ today. Those who explain it away say, "It is heavenly living." or "It is only for self-righteous Jews," or "It is only for clergy."

Those who attempt to *explain* it have offered an equally wide variety of interpretations. They say: the commands are absolute (must be obeyed), or the commands apply only to attitude (not action), or the commands are impossible to obey (they are to lead a lost person to faith in Christ for the free gift).

The most common explanation offered today is the latter: the sermon is laying out an impossible standard so that lost people are led to faith in Christ for His gift of righteousness. Yet the standards, under this line of reasoning, become the necessary proof of a person's salvation. Absence of these standards, according to this view, proves a person either lost his salvation or never really had it to begin with.

Why all this confusion?

The confusion is because these attempts have thought the sermon was about getting to heaven. All of these attempts ignore the simple and natural reading of the sermon and miss the powerful point Jesus was making.

These attempts not only ignore the plain meaning, they are dangerous!

Why are they dangerous?

The danger in making the sermon about getting to heaven is that it is impossible to get away from good works as a condition of salvation either as a means or as a proof.

Good works are never a means or proof of your eternal standing.

Good works by themselves are never a means or a proof of your eternal standing with God. As Dr. Charles Bing strongly states, "There is no passage of Scripture that claims works can prove salvation."[9]

If good works are an absolute and definitive proof, we are all in serious trouble and destined to an insecure, unsure, futile, and legalistic life, which this sermon warns against!

CLEARING UP THE CONFUSION: JESUS' AUDIENCE

How do those who say this sermon is about heaven arrive at this conclusion? The first mistake made is a blurring of the distinction between the kingdom of heaven and heaven. If the kingdom of heaven and heaven are the same thing, then by looking at what Jesus said, it is clear that good works are required to get us into heaven.[10]

But that totally nullifies grace.[11]

The first step to properly understanding the plain, natural meaning of this sermon is to identify the historical audience. Discussion has been fairly exhaustive on this issue, but the general debate is whether the "disciples"[12] or the "multitudes"[13] are the direct addressees. While both groups are affected by the sermon, it must be established which group is the direct addressees.

It is the disciples that "came to Him"[14]; then it says, "he began to teach them."[15] If this is not evidence enough, then the overwhelming evidence that the sermon is addressed to Jesus' disciples, who almost assuredly must be identified as the Twelve, is affirmed in the sermon itself. Within the sermon we find that the addressees are:[16]

Those who *have God as their Father* (stated 16 times),[17]

Those who were already salt and light,[18]

Those who may be persecuted for King Jesus' sake,[19]

Those who can love "perfect" as God loves perfectly,[20]

Those who labor for rewards, not redemption,[21]

Those who can pray to God as their heavenly Father,[22]

Those who trust God to provide their needs,[23]

Those who should expect answers to their prayers,[24] and

Those who have desire and means to identify false prophets.[25]

The only natural and reasonable conclusion is that the addressees are the disciples: saved individuals who have committed to follow Jesus.

The Sermon on the Mount, then, is addressed to "saved" people.

Now, on to the next point of confusion.

CLEARING UP CONFUSION: A KINGDOM

It is universally accepted that the Sermon on the Mount is about a kingdom, as is indicated by the fact that the word exists eight times within the three chapters. Both Matthew 5:20 and 6:33, considered good purpose statements for the sermon, call its readers to a kingdom:

> For I say to you that unless your righteousness surpasses that of the scribes and Pharisees, you will not enter the kingdom of heaven.[26]

> But seek first His kingdom and His righteousness, and all these things will be added to you.[27]

The controversial question is not about whether the sermon is about a kingdom, but whether this kingdom is a spiritual kingdom, a reference to heaven or to salvation in general, or whether it refers to the anticipated, literal, Messianic kingdom of David's promised seed. What you choose here is critical to the whole sermon and to some degree to the rest of the New Testament as well.

The previous instance of the word *kingdom* prior to this sermon is in the description of the message Jesus was proclaiming throughout all Galilee.[28] Once again it is helpful to remember that "the background of the New Testament idea of the kingdom must be found in the Old Testament."[29] And as we have seen previously, "It is a well established fact that the Jews at the time of Christ were anticipating a literal fulfillment of the promises of the Old Testament, theocratic kingdom."[30]

We should not, therefore, change the meaning of the term kingdom unless some change in meaning is offered by Jesus or the writer of the Gospel himself. Since no such indication is given, in an effort to be consistent, we must accept that the Sermon on the

Mount is about the earthly Messianic kingdom, not about heaven or eternal salvation. It was suggested in the last chapter that the term *heaven* describes the kingdom's origination and quality, not its locale. The same is true here in the Sermon on the Mount.

The Sermon on the Mount is about the literal earthly reign of Messiah.

CLEARING UP CONFUSION: RIGHTEOUSNESS

Another mistake is the blurring of the distinction between positional righteousness and practical righteousness. Think about those two words: positional and practical.

When I think of positional, I think about a position, status or standing. If I am born in the U.S.A. then I am an American. My status is legal, but in order to live free to pursue the American dream I must live like an American practically speaking. When I live like an American, practically, I enjoy the benefits of my status.

I may choose to live disconnected from society and exclude myself from the benefits, but my status has not changed; I am still an American. My practice changed, but my position remained the same.

Biblically speaking practical righteousness refers to an individual's acts of righteousness; positional righteousness refers to my standing before God as either saved or not saved on the basis of the imputed righteousness of Jesus that is accredited to our accounts legally where He declares a person justified, legally acquitted from all guilt and condemnation.[31]

By blurring these two different kinds of righteousness, the good works in the Sermon on the Mount are made a requirement for salvation. The Pauline doctrine of imputed righteousness, however, is not even discussed in the entire book of Matthew. The righteousness referred to in the Gospel of Matthew is practical; it describes what a person actually does in the responses that he makes toward God.[32]

In the middle of the sermon, Jesus told the disciples to "beware of practicing your righteousness before men to be noticed by them."[33] Here righteousness must be a reference to the right actions required from God's people and not to a positional or legal righteousness that cannot be demonstrated in any way. The righteousness in this context is identified as giving, as God has commanded believers to do, offering prayers to God according to God's instructions, and fasting until Jesus returns.

It is practical righteousness that qualifies a person for his treasure in the kingdom. Good works are the condition for the kingdom. To realize greatness in the kingdom one must meet the practical demands.[34]

TO ENTER IN

Those conditions necessary to enter the kingdom and realize greatness[35] are spelled out in the sermon. They are good character,[36] fulfillment of a godly calling,[37] and godly conduct for the glory of God.[38] The point of the warning at the end of the sermon ("I never knew you; DEPART FROM ME,"[39]), misused by so many, clearly conveys that doing the right thing alone won't get a person into the kingdom to be great. For this a person must do the right thing in the right way. It must be godly conduct, defined in this sermon as doing the right thing from a right heart for the glory of God.

Jesus gave the sermon to His disciples (not the unsaved), and to all future believers by way of application, to give the conditions necessary to participate in the coming kingdom. This sermon was meant to fan the flame of each believer's faith to lead him to zealously pursue the kingdom.[40]

What are the critical points here? What things must we make sure we don't miss, or mix up?

- The Sermon on the Mount is addressed to "saved" individuals and therefore applicable to the church.

- The kingdom talked about in the Sermon on the Mount is not a spiritual kingdom, heaven, nor salvation. It is the literal coming kingdom of Christ.

- The Sermon on the Mount is not about salvation, since it was not given to the lost. It was spoken for the saved to instruct them about how to enter into that coming kingdom of Christ.

- The righteousness that is talked about is not positional (justification—the issue of eternal salvation), but rather practical (works), required by God for participation in the coming kingdom of Christ.

The condition for entrance into the kingdom, then, is a practical "righteousness [that] surpasses that of the scribes and Pharisees."[41] This righteousness is not already possessed by saved individuals. This righteousness must be hungered and thirsted for;[42] it is something that brings persecution upon us;[43] it is something that is done,[44] as well as something to be sought by the believer.[45] The whole sermon is an explanation of that practical righteousness which must be superior to and surpass that of the inadequate, improperly motivated, fleshly, and hypocritical righteousness of the scribes and Pharisees.

SURPASSING RIGHTEOUSNESS

In the Sermon on the Mount Jesus explains plainly what the entrance requirements for the literal Messianic kingdom are to realize greatness. To summarize the requirements we could simply refer to Matthew 5:20—a person's practical righteousness must surpass that of the scribes and Pharisees. Ugh!

While both the scribes and Pharisees were externally righteous, the original intention of the Law was to address the heart since it is the originating source of all our actions, both our sin as well as our obedience.

So, what does the surpassing practical righteousness look like?

Practical righteousness that surpasses the scribes and Pharisees is seen in godly character.

The first portion of the sermon (5:3–12) gives clear examples of the kind of character needed. Anyone who wishes to earn rewards and share in the Messianic kingdom on earth must be submissive and dependent upon God; he must be poor in spirit. He must be able to control his strength, strive to do God's will, be patient and forgiving (merciful), clean hearted, a peacemaker, and totally committed to Christ.

To be a person of this character does not mean that one needs to be perfect in order to enter and share in the kingdom; it means that these traits characterize his life.

Practical righteousness that surpasses the scribes and Pharisees is seen in the realization of a godly calling.

We have all been called to preserve and season the world with the salt of God's grace and truth. And we are called to be the visible examples and reflectors of the "Light of the world."[46] God had always desired the nation of Israel to be salt and light, but their privileged position went to their heads, and they became self-righteous, thinking they were superior to the rest of the world. In order to surpass their religious righteousness, we need to function consistently as God made us; we are salt and light, and should desire to fulfill those roles for the glory of God.

Practical righteousness that surpasses the scribes and Pharisees is measured by the quality of the right acts which are done.

While we are not under the Law today,[47] at the time the sermon was given by Jesus, the Law was the revealed will of God. The principles discussed are repeated throughout the New Testament and become a part of the Law of Christ[48] performed by Christ's life in us through faith and not by our own effort.[49]

The point here is the intent of the Law. The intent of the

Law, and any command of Scripture, is to address our hearts so that our obedience to God represents the whole man, not merely conforming to an external religious order. Consequently, the intent of the command *you shall not murder* was to restrain our hearts from hating one another.

The intent of the command *You shall not commit adultery* was to restrain our hearts from being dissatisfied with the wife of our youth[50] and looking for another instead.[51] The intent of the command *You shall not make false vows* was to restrain our hearts from being wishy-washy with our words.

The intent of the command *An eye for an eye* was to prevent individual, personal retribution. Instead, we are all called to be gracious, and let the systems in place take care of justice. The intent of the command *You shall love your neighbor* was to challenge believers to be complete in their love just as the Father is complete in His. He loves the unlovable and so should we if we want to enter the kingdom with our full inheritance.

The righteousness that surpasses the scribes and Pharisees designates right acts done from a proper motivation.

The motivation of the scribes and Pharisees was completely self-centered. What they did was for their own glory. A practical righteousness that surpasses theirs constitutes right acts done for the glory and honor of God who repays the obedience with rewards that pertain to kingdom living and privileges.

Living with the wrong motivation is the antithesis of living by faith. Faith always leads to the glory of God because faith depends upon God. Faith makes His attributes known in such a way that He gets the credit.

We should always do the right thing in dependence upon God, knowing that if we seek His kingdom and His righteousness, He will take care of our basic temporal needs. When we live for the kingdom, we won't worry about tomorrow for God will certainly take care of that.[52] He can be trusted, and should be trusted.

A practical righteousness that surpasses the scribes and Pharisees manifests itself in non-hypocritical living.

We simply cannot have a standard for others that we ourselves are not willing to live under. We cannot expect others to live lives to the glory of God if we are not willing to be responsible to remove the logs from our own eyes.[53] We must become people who are willing to live by the Golden Rule.[54]

A practical righteousness that surpasses that of the scribes and Pharisees means that we must seek to enter the kingdom by the "narrow gate."[55] Jesus has provided the narrow way in this sermon. If we give the right responses in the wrong way, no matter how religious we look, when it comes time to enter the kingdom and obtain our inheritance Jesus will say to us, "Depart...I never knew you"[56] (the "knowing" is an issue of intimacy in the practice of those things He desired). They did the right things, but they did them the wrong way.

While our eternal destiny with God, our eternal salvation, never comes into jeopardy, our participation in the inheritance in the coming kingdom certainly will. We were chosen and called for this end; we must not miss it.

The only way to enter the kingdom with our full inheritance is by living under the lordship of Jesus Christ, as we turn our hearts toward Him, submit ourselves to Him, love that which He loves, and live for His glory. This is the substance of the sermon.

PLAIN SENSE HAS MEAT

"When the plain sense makes sense, look for no other sense."

If my wife leaves me a note and says that she will meet me at the school at six, I know plainly that this means she will meet me at the school my kids attend at six o'clock in the evening (for she is not a morning person!). That is the plain sense as it was intended and received. If she leaves me a note that asks me to pick up some bread and milk for the kids, I not only know that bread means bread and milk means milk; I also know that it means potato bread and 2 percent milk because it is for the kids. (If it were for me, it would be skim milk and whole wheat bread. I need all the help I can get!)

When the plain sense makes sense, look for no other sense.

When we interpret this great sermon literally within the historical context, the sermon makes total sense.

The principles and application made sense for the disciples, and they should make sense for the believer today. We should expect that on a topic as important as the coming Messianic kingdom Jesus would give a clear, sensible teaching on how to get there so as not to miss the narrow gate. Otherwise we may be wasting our lives.

To miss the glorious intention of this sermon is to miss the glorious nature and wisdom of our Father who is heaven.

TO GUIDE AND DIRECT

As a father of two boys, I take away great parenting insight from the Sermon on the Mount. The older they get the more creative I must be in order to lovingly discipline them or motivate them to do the right thing and become men of character. They are too big to put over my knee anymore, so I must find things they value and use those levers as reward or consequence. I would be utterly ineffective if I chose something they do not really care about, for it would lack meaning and significance to them; it would not motivate them in the least.

Our heavenly Father has created us to rule, and He, therefore, uses the kingdom as a reward to motivate us and lovingly discipline us to be kids that live for His glory. Never once have I communicated to my children that the loss of a reward also jeopardizes my love for them or my commitment to them. I learned that from my heavenly Father as well.

Since this sermon makes it plainly obvious that good works done the right way are essential for greatness in the kingdom, we not only relieve ourselves of the burdensome theology that casts doubt on the great grace of God, but we also liberate ourselves to live according to this newfound freedom and motivation. The way is broad to "destruction";[57] a wasted life, but Jesus does not want us to miss the narrow gate. Living a moral or religious life will prove insufficient for the kingdom.

The Sermon on the Mount provides our marching orders and the plan of attack...seek the kingdom!

Enter by the narrow gate.

NOTES

1 Matthew 7:13.

2 William F. Arndt, F. Wilbur Gingrich, and Walter Bauer, *A Greek-English Lexicon of the New Testament and Other Early Christian Literature*, (Chicago: University of Chicago Press, 1979), 2nd ed.,103.

3 Matthew 26:8, emphasis mine.

4 Matthew 7:13.

5 Matthew 7:14.

6 Matthew 5:19, 20.

7 Matthew 3:2; 4:23.

8 Compare the chronology of the accounts of Matthew and Luke.

9 Charles C. Bing, *Simply by Grace: An Introduction to God's Life-Changing Gift* (Grand Rapids, MI: Kregel Pubications, 2009), 85.

10 Matthew 7:21.

11 Romans 11:6; Galatians 2:21.

12 Matthew 5:1–2.

13 Matthew 5:1; 7:28.

14 Mathew 5:1.

15 Matthew 5:2.

16 Dr. B. Dale Taliaferro, "Gospel of Matthew" (unpublished notes).

17 Matthew 5:16, 45, 48; 6:1, 4, 6 (twice), 8, 9, 14, 15, 18 (twice), 26, 32; 7:11.

18 Matthew 5:13–14.

19 Matthew 5:10–11.

20 Matthew 5:48.

21 Matthew 6:1–21.

22 Matthew 6:9.

23 Matthew 6:25–34.

24 Matthew 7:7–11.

25 Matthew 7:15–20; Deuteronomy 13:1–4.

26 Matthew 5:20.

27 Matthew 6:33.

28 Matthew 4:23.

29 McClain, *The Greatness of the Kingdom*, 19.

30 Pentecost, *Thy Kingdom Come*, 446.

31 See 2 Corinthians 5:21.

32 Matthew 3:15 is a clear example for Jesus did not need legal righteousness; see 21:32 for the other case outside of the Sermon on the Mount.

33 See Matthew 6:1.

34 See Matthew 5:19.

35 See Matthew 5:19.

36 See Matthew 5:3–12.

37 See Matthew 5:13–16.

38 See Matthew 5:17–7:27.

39 Matthew 7:23.

40 Matthew 6:33.

41 Matthew 5:20.

42 See Matthew 5:6.

43 See Matthew 5:10.

44 See Matthew 6:1.

45 See Matthew 6:33.

46 John 8:12.

47 See Romans 6:14; 7:1–6; Ephesians 2:14–15.

48 See Galatians 6:2; see also the law of liberty in James 1:25.

49 See 2 Corinthians 5:7; Galatians 2:20; 3:1–3; Hebrews 11:6.

50 See Proverbs 5:18; Ecclesiastes 9:9.

51 Looking is one thing (we may not be able to help that), but looking in a way that communicates a real desire is to add a purpose to the look that is unrighteous.

52 See Matthew 6:34.

53 See Matthew 7:1–6.

54 See Matthew 7:12.

55 See Matthew 7:13.

56 See Matthew 7:21–23.

57 The word *destruction* is defined as "trifling away one's life" (Gerhard Kittel, *Theological Dictionary of the New Testament,* vol. 1 [Grand Rapids, MI: Wm. B. Eerdmans Publishing Company, 1964], 394).

ELEVEN

TREASURE
IN MYSTERIES

*Truth is the property of no individual
but is the treasure of all men.*

Ralph Waldo Emerson

My family really enjoys mystery adventure films. One of
our family favorites is the *National Treasure* series with
Nicholas Cage. These films are about a group of mystery adventure
hunters unraveling national mysteries that have never been solved or
proven; and often they are working to disprove a theory which has
been widely accepted as fact, though more conjecture was present
than evidence. It is captivating and exciting to see how one clue
after another leads to the unlocking of these historical mysteries
and amazing treasure.

And who doesn't like to find treasure?

At a fairly early point in Jesus' ministry, due to the mounting
rejection He was facing, especially after the religious leaders

accused Him of doing Satan's work, Jesus began to unfold mysteries of the kingdom. These mysteries were things God knew but had not previously made known. While prophets of old and righteous men sought this information,[1] God was preserving its revealing for just the right time. In the continuum of Jesus' ministry the time was...now.

Unraveling these mysteries of the kingdom is captivating and exciting because it leads to priceless treasure: greater understanding of God and His kingdom program.

Back to *National Treasure* for a moment.

I love the part in the movie when Benjamin Franklin Gates, played by Nicholas Cage, goes up the steeple of Liberty Hall (where the Liberty Bell once hung) at exactly 2:20 p.m. to get the next clue. From his vantage point in the steeple he notices the shadow the steeple casts on a neighboring building's brick wall. Upon approaching this wall, he discovers a single brick with a Free Masons symbol on it; in that brick Gates finds the next clue. What led him to this brick was the vantage point he gained from the steeple in the Liberty Hall which gave a new perspective to find this clue.

And that's what it's all about: vantage point. When we look at passages in Scripture, we need to look at them from the vantage point that gives us the best overall perspective; we need to view passages, or in this case parables, against the whole of Scripture and keeping the context of the times in mind. If we don't, we have no vantage point and miss the big picture...and possibly the treasure.

UNDERSTANDING PARABLES

Here are a few things to remember about parables:

- A parable is a story cast alongside an important teaching which uses a "common event of natural life to emphasize or clarify an important spiritual truth."[2]

- The historical and textual context provides the point the parable intends to shed light upon.

- A parable has a central point and oftentimes many details that relate to and support that central point. While the details are helpful they are "not to be given meaning that is independent of the main teaching of the parable."[3]

These are all helpful reminders that will aid us in effectively interpreting the parables and seeing the mysteries that were revealed.

When Jesus spoke in parables, as here in Matthew 13, He used common things around Him to convey ideas and communicate concepts/truths. As we look at what Jesus said in these parables, it is important to apply the historical context that Jesus and the disciples were in so that we understand the mysteries according to how they were meant to be understood.

On this occasion, following His rejection by the Pharisees, Jesus spoke the first parable and the disciples asked Him why He chose to speak in this parabolic manner.[4] Jesus explained that in this case a parable served two primary purposes: (1) to reveal truth to the receptive; and (2) to conceal it from the unreceptive.[5] Thus, these parables are quite unique and specific to the historical setting.

UNRAVELING THE MYSTERIES

Once again...briefly back to the movie.

Benjamin Franklin Gates, the lead role in *National Treasure*, has an uncanny ability to uncover clues to the mysteries he encounters, almost as if he has some foreknowledge or sixth sense of what the answers to the mysteries were. Jesus told the disciples that they had already been granted to know the mysteries of the kingdom,[6] but to the multitudes it had not been so granted.[7] Even though the disciples asked for explanations[8] the capacity to understand was theirs that very day. The "cat is out of the bag"; the mysterious information was, and now is, revealed.

Our task is to rightly interpret these mysteries in the ancient text and rightly apply them to our lives.

Now, to the mysteries.

The matter that Jesus is illustrating is said to be "mysteries of the kingdom."[9] The word *mystery* means something known only by direct revelation; it refers not only to something that had "previously not been revealed (secrets), but also to the mysterious and not independently knowable nature of what has now been made known."[10]

Most importantly, these mysteries being revealed by Jesus are about "*the* kingdom."[11] It is not the kingdom itself which is the mystery; the mysteries are *about* the kingdom.

And, nowhere in the chapter is there any indication that the kingdom being discussed is a different kingdom than the coming kingdom of Christ, which had previously been proclaimed and taught. Nor is there any indication that these mysteries are describing a mystery form of a new kingdom. Despite some popular interpretations, these parables which Jesus taught were not His way of introducing a new *spiritual* form of the kingdom called the church.

The most fluid and consistent interpretation is that the kingdom being discussed is the literal earthly kingdom of Messiah. Each parable teaches valuable lessons about God's Messianic kingdom program.

The principle of interpretation discussed in previous chapters applies here in the same fashion it does elsewhere. Kingdom must mean what the author meant and those hearing understood. As we have seen before "the background of the New Testament idea of the kingdom must be found in the Old Testament."[12] With no indication of change in meaning, it is incumbent upon the reader to be consistent in the interpretation of these terms according to their prior usage.

Why is this important?

Because we must understand the original intent of the parables; otherwise, we miss the truth as it was intended altogether. The mysteries are mysteries of *the* earthly kingdom of Messiah. Jesus speaking in parables does not indicate that He has abandoned His Kingdom promise or given up on the crowds or the nation of Israel.

But it certainly "makes a public statement [about the crowds] that they remain outsiders to what God is currently doing."[13]

With proper use of the principles of interpretation we can conclude:

- The mysteries are truths about the literal kingdom of Messiah, which were not previously discussed in the Old Testament.

- Jesus is not teaching a new form of the kingdom, He is giving more information about the kingdom being offered and is certain to come.

- The mysteries were given to the disciples to be understood and applied to their lives prior to the inception of the church and the principles will be applicable even after the church is gone; until "the end of the age."[14]

It is worthy of notice that *after* Jesus taught the disciples the mysteries of the kingdom, their concept of the kingdom as being the earthly kingdom of Messiah remained the same. His disciples were still seeking to be great in the coming kingdom[15] and still thought the kingdom could appear when Jesus drew near to Jerusalem.[16] Even after Jesus' death and resurrection, their expectation was for a literal kingdom of Messiah for Israel.[17]

One additional support for this being about a literal kingdom is seen in the fact that Jesus told the disciples that many prophets and righteous men wanted to see and hear what Jesus was telling the disciples, but they were unable.[18] Certainly prophets and righteous men of the Old Testament would have sought information on the kingdom revealed, not a new form of the kingdom not yet revealed.

Finally the application of the truths being revealed will be true until the "end of the age; at the time of the harvest."[19] These parables were given before the first mention of the church,[20] and the inception of the church after Jesus' ascension.[21] Thus these parables demand applicability until the second coming of Messiah to establish His kingdom on earth.

The mysteries are, therefore, not about the church as a new *form* of kingdom.

> *The mysteries are not about the church as a new form of kingdom.*

The application was true for the disciples, it is applicable to the church, and it will be applicable for the saints during the Tribulation.

We should not confuse these "mysteries of the kingdom" with the later writing of Paul on the church, which was certainly a mystery not previously revealed in the Old Testament.[22] Paul defines *that* mystery for us:

Gentiles are fellow heirs and fellow members of the body, and fellow partakers of the promise in Christ Jesus.[23]

One mystery does not equate to another even if some principles may be similar. Paul never indicates that the church is a kingdom, which we will explore later, but for now we must interpret these mysteries in light of their historical context.

These mysteries of the kingdom make perfect sense in light of the historical context of Jesus' public ministry and we should therefore not look for any alternative, ethereal meaning.

THE PARABLES OF JESUS

Here in Central Oregon it is winter right now. The trees are bare, the grass is brown, and the days are short (not at all good for my golf game). But now that we've passed the winter equinox, the days are gradually getting longer and I know that spring will be coming soon. I know that underneath that solidly frozen soil, there are grass seeds readying themselves to break through, and dormant tree roots waiting for the warmth of the sun to stimulate them to grow.

The process of the grass, plants, and trees awakening in spring begins where we cannot see: under the soil. But once the process is in full swing, we can all see the evidence of its hidden workings. There may have been some evidence as the time drew near, like soil bulging before a sprig sprouts up, but not until that sprig shoots upwards and bears a bright red flower does it express the fullness of its essence.

As you study the parables of Jesus from Matthew 13, keep these concepts in mind:

- There are "preparatory works" being done "under the soil" before the kingdom will come (which was not something that the Jews of the time of Jesus understood). Nonetheless this is an important aspect of His kingdom.

- The parables are about the coming kingdom, which will be glorious and is worth everything.

- The kingdom's coming is certain, absolute, and not to be doubted

- Good and evil will coexist until the end of the age (at the end of the Tribulation), at which time Christ will judge and separate them, and the righteous will enter the kingdom.

Now the first of eight parables.

SOWER AND THE SOILS[24]

THE TALE: A sower goes out to sow seed in his field. Some seeds fall along the road through his field; some fall in rocky ground; other seeds fall in weedy soil; and some fall into good soil. The fruitfulness of the seeds sown is determined by the soil into which they fall. Some bears no fruit; some bears fruit temporarily; and good soil bears fruit thirty, sixty, and one hundred times the fruit of the others.

This first parable illustrates four different responses to the kingdom message Jesus proclaims. The parable gives the reason that someone can hear the word of the kingdom yet "not understand it."[25] This is one of the eight parables which Jesus gives explanation[26]; and He defines the *seed* as the "word of the kingdom."[27]

The roadside soil represents a person who does not understand because "the evil one comes and snatches away what has been sown in his heart."[28] Satan finds some to be easy targets and steals the word of the kingdom from their heart before they can truly benefit from the life changing message/offer.

In the parallel account in Luke, Luke adds the statement "so that they will not believe and be saved."[29] It is not the intention of Luke to make this parable about eternal salvation since the historical context is the same as Matthew's and is therefore about the kingdom, not eternal salvation.[30] The salvation is Messianic or kingdom related, as previously noted. To not be saved is to miss the kingdom. This parable, like the rest here, is not about going to heaven, as many have taught and believed; it is about the messianic kingdom.

The rocky soil represents a shallow person who is initially thrilled about the word of the kingdom. However, the persecution that comes on account of that word causes him to fall away from having a full understanding that leads to bearing fruit. Here the persecution that comes is that which adversely affects understanding the kingdom privileges being offered.

The weed infested soil is the distracted worldly person who won't give the word time to grow and bear fruit in his life. "The worry of the world and the deceitfulness of wealth" work adversely against the message of the kingdom, and the shallow person "becomes unfruitful."[31]

The good soil, the last of the four, represents the person who understands the word of the kingdom and bears fruit. The fruit is an indication that in the right person the word of the kingdom will "show itself splendidly fruitful."[32] These are the ones, like the disciples, that are getting the message and are responding appropriately.

This parable fits perfectly within the historical context of Jesus' rejection to this point, because it shows that Israel's rejection is a matter of personal responsibility. The reason why Israel's response to Christ was inadequate was because their hearts were dull of hearing![33] The Old Testament did not reveal that Israel would be unreceptive to Messiah. In fact, the Old Testament emphasized their receptivity[34] and repentant spiritual enthusiasm.[35]

What is being revealed here is that Jesus is developing a following, not delivering a nation, through the word of the kingdom. Three out of the four soils reject or bear no fruit; the fourth, however, has experienced life change and bears fruit, and he tells others the word (here the parallel to the parable of the head of household is clear).

The application of the parable of the sower and the soils should move us to sow the word of the kingdom indiscriminately in the world. Jesus clearly taught that we are to make disciples, not just converts, of every nation by baptizing them and teaching them to obey all that He commanded.[36] We are not here to simply make converts to Jesus; we are here to make those converts into fully devoted disciples who live for the kingdom.

Since only certain soils will be receptive to the word of the kingdom, we must cultivate the soil of our own hearts and the hearts of those we journey alongside. But what is certain is that the seed that is sown by the sower will be fruitful in the right soil.

The parable also serves as a warning as to the forces that are at work against the kingdom message. Satan is definitely an adversary of the kingdom, but so too are persecution, worry, and materialism. We need to guard against all of these things that work against the word of the kingdom and producing fruit in the lives of those who hear.

WHEAT AND TARES OF THE FIELD[37]

THE TALE: The kingdom of heaven is like a man who sowed good seed in his field. During the night his enemy sows tares in the same field. After the wheat and tares bear grain, it becomes obvious that tares are mixed in with the wheat; yet servants are directed to allow the tares to grow for fear of uprooting some of the wheat. The tares and the wheat are allowed to grow together until harvest time (the end of the age), at which point the tares are gathered and burned up, and the wheat is gathered and stored in the landowner's barn.

This is the second parable of the eight for which Jesus gave the disciples an explanation.[38] Jesus explained that the man who sows good seed is the "Son of Man," a title that has obvious Messianic implication:

> Jesus is referred to as the "Son of Man" 88 times in the New Testament. A first meaning of the phrase "Son of Man" is as a reference to the prophecy of Daniel 7:13–14...and was a Messianic title. Jesus is the One who was given dominion and glory and a kingdom. When Jesus used this phrase, He was assigning the Son of Man prophecy to Himself. The Jews of that era would have been intimately familiar with the phrase and to whom it referred. Jesus was proclaiming Himself as the Messiah.[39]

In His earthly ministry Jesus was sowing the good seed. Jesus also explains the field is the world, not the church.[40] The good seed are the sons of the kingdom, and the tares are the sons of the evil one, the devil. The sons of the kingdom is the nation of Israel;[41] these are the sons to whom the kingdom belonged. The harvest is the end of the age where sons of the kingdom and the sons of the evil one will be separated from one another and only the sons of the kingdom remain to inhabit the earth during His reign.[42]

This parable illustrates:

- The certainty of His coming kingdom in spite of Israel's rejection.

- What the preparatory work will look like (good and evil side by side) until that kingdom is established.

- That good and evil will be allowed to coexist until the time of the harvest at the end of the age.

- That it is not the job of the servants of the kingdom to separate good and evil (which won't be distinct until "wheat sprouted and bore grain"[43]).

- That the mystery being revealed is the process that the Son of Man will use to produce a righteous population to inherit the kingdom.

While the goal and final nature of the kingdom when it comes is discussed in the Old Testament,[44] the preparatory process between His first coming and second was not. While Jesus is at the right hand of the Father until He comes again to set up His kingdom,[45] He nevertheless continues to be personally involved in the work to "the end of the age."[46]

During this preparatory process, the devil will continue his present reign of evil, which will not be the case during the earthly reign of Messiah.[47] During the present age, evil will exist right alongside the good and will not always be distinct and should not be dealt with by means of separation. The separation will take place by the angels at the end of the age.[48] While evil will exist today, God will not act decisively until the time of harvest. This is an important part of the overall kingdom program today, but the emphasis is still on the certainty of the kingdom to come.[49]

The parable of the *wheat and tares* teaches us that until Jesus comes back we are not always going to know by external appearance who are the wheat and who are the tares—not until the time of the harvest, when the wheat bears grain and the tares show their ugly heads. For this reason we should not condemn anyone on the basis of outward appearance. If we persist in this vein we will undoubtedly uproot some good wheat. God will take care of all judgment. He can be trusted to sort it all out.

Our tendency is to develop a list of what we think a good Christian looks like and piously judge according to that list who is and who is not a genuine believer. In doing this, we have created so many problems for ourselves and others by setting up an ideal that is impossible to live up to; it is an ideal that never gives the assurance of our security in God's love.

This parable teaches us that the preparatory work leading up to the kingdom will be one that needs to be patiently and faithfully endured. But make no mistake: the seed is sown, and continues, and one day "THE RIGHTEOUS WILL SHINE FORTH AS THE SUN in the kingdom of their Father."[50] God will have a righteous population to inherit and populate the kingdom.

MUSTARD SEED[51]

THE TALE: The kingdom of heaven is like a mustard seed. Although the mustard seed is smaller than the other seeds in a garden, once sown by a man in his field it will produce a tree larger than other garden plants, large enough for birds to nest in its branches.

This parable about the smallest seed illustrates that despite the fact that the kingdom preparations look small and insignificant, like a mustard seed they will grow exponentially, into a magnificent tree. That fully developed tree will be adequate for the establishment of the kingdom, like birds nesting in its mighty branches.

The seed is already sown and the final outcome of the full-grown tree is certain. The Old Testament does not reveal this preparatory work, that which happens below the soil, but only describes the kingdom as all encompassing, even cataclysmic, at the triumphant second coming of Christ.[52] The current work is part of the kingdom and is essential to its future establishment. As John Nolland comments,

> As God can be trusted with the potential in a planted seed, so he can be trusted with the potential set loose by the ministry of Jesus. What is happening in Jesus' presence makes certain the future (full) coming of the kingdom, precisely because the life of that future kingdom is already making itself manifest...the parable is about confidence rather than process.[53]

The confidence is that what Jesus began will certainly come to pass in the future.

The parable of the *mustard seed* teaches us that we should never get discouraged in our spiritual efforts and pursuits, though in the world's eyes they may seem small and insignificant. Everything we do today, regardless of size, is being used in the preparatory work of Christ and His kingdom.

One of the important roles we play in this preparatory work is in our relationship with the lost world, who do not yet believe Christ and have failed to understand the word of the kingdom. As we grow into a huge mustard tree, when we are "caught up together with Christ in the air,"[54] the relationships you have lovingly fostered here will make your absence felt by those who are left behind. When we are caught up together with Christ in the air I hope people will notice we are gone and realize the truth of what we believed.

LEAVEN[55]

THE TALE: The kingdom of heaven is like leaven. A woman places leaven in three lumps of meal and the leavening process continues until all is leavened.

The parable of the leaven illustrates the fact that the present ministry of Jesus is like leaven hidden in the meal, which will reproduce in the certainty of the kingdom to come. While the ministry of Jesus made little visible difference, the process had begun and the outcome is certain. The small amount of leaven is hidden in a large amount of dough in the same way that the word of the kingdom was, and would be, sown into a large audience.

This organic preparatory work was not previously revealed in the Old Testament, but it will continue till the end of the age when it is completely leavened.[56] The final outcome of the kingdom is certain and inevitable since the leaven had been hidden through the ministry and death of Jesus the Christ. This is yet another illustration of what God is doing to raise up a righteous remnant for the future kingdom.

The parable of the *leaven* ought to remind us that, while the work today seems to be going along rather slowly, the end is definite, for God will certainly set up His kingdom with a righteous remnant. The preparatory work today has a certain outcome because of the nature of the work itself and who began it.

HIDDEN TREASURE[57]

THE TALE: The kingdom is compared to a hidden treasure. A man finds the treasure hidden in a field that does not belong to him, so he sells all he owns to buy the field and possess the treasure.

The parable of the hidden treasure illustrates the value of the kingdom and the sacrifice necessary to obtain it. The mystery being revealed is that the glory of the kingdom is even greater than described in the Old Testament, and that

> *If we want treasure, we must seek the kingdom.*

the condition for its possession is sacrifice. While the Old Testament reveals a great description of the kingdom, it does not reveal the condition of sacrifice necessary for possession of it as reward.

Living for the kingdom is how we better ourselves.

If we want treasure, we must seek the kingdom.[58] What a fortune all will find who discover the value of the kingdom!

MERCHANT AND THE PEARL OF GREAT PRICE[59]

THE TALE: The kingdom of heaven is like a merchant seeking fine pearls. Upon finding a pearl of great value, the merchant sells all he owns to buy it.

This parable is quite similar to the parable of the hidden treasure and illustrates that the kingdom is worth investing all you have in order to obtain it. Possession of the kingdom will be based on stewardship, not merely genealogy. This too was not revealed in the Old Testament.

The parables of the *hidden treasure* and *the pearl of great price* teach us of the importance of the glorious coming kingdom of Christ. The glorious kingdom is worth every sacrifice necessary to obtain it. While eternal salvation is a gift from God which we receive freely by faith alone, the kingdom is something to be obtained by faithful stewardship and sacrifice. The action required, the sacrifices demanded, are little in comparison to the value of the prize: the kingdom.

Seek the kingdom and His righteousness.[60] It is worth it!

DRAG NET[61]

THE TALE: The kingdom of heaven is like a dragnet cast into the sea. The net gathers fish of every kind and is dragged up to the beach to separate the good fish from the bad fish. The bad fish are thrown away, and the good fish are kept.

The parable of the dragnet illustrates that the preparatory work of the kingdom is like a large net cast into the sea which gathers fish of every kind. The purpose of the dragnet is to catch all it can. Concern should not be about discriminating between what is caught. The discrimination of good and evil will come at the end of the age when the kingdom will begin. At that time the good and bad fish, which represent the righteous and the wicked, will be separated from one another at "the end of the age."[62] The emphasis in this parable is on the fate of the catch and the sorting at the end of the age.

The parable of the *dragnet* teaches us that God is very intentional about getting as many people to the kingdom as possible and He is not immediately concerned about discrimination.

The parable of the dragnet emphasizes the "fate of the catch" (not the activity of the fishermen). It is a harvest at the end of the age! The only time for sorting is the end of the age. We don't have to worry about who will get in or who won't; we need to just keep doing what we are called to do and let the net fill. The preparatory kingdom work is the process not described but easily imagined: the net is getting full of all sorts!

HEAD OF A HOUSEHOLD[63]

THE TALE: The disciple of the kingdom of heaven is like a head of a household. The head of the household is one who brings out good things (treasure) old and new to benefit others.

This final parable illustrates that being a disciple of the

kingdom of heaven requires them to maintain their perspective and anticipation of the kingdom described in the Old Testament (as a scribe would), but also being teachable enough to accept new enlightenments of that same kingdom from these mysteries.

The parable of the *head of the household* teaches us that a disciple, in every generation, needs to be serious about the study of the whole Bible, both Old and New Testaments. The Old Testament is the foundation and the New Testament builds upon it; both are essential to our kingdom perspective. If we do this, the kingdom will be a central focus of our lives and ministry.

The treasure a disciple earns is also treasure he ought to share with others.

GREAT TREASURE

In the movie *National Treasure*, Ben Gates is unraveling mysteries in search of the greatest historical collection of treasure ever, and in the process vindicating his family name. Clue after clue leads Gates closer and closer until finally he is at the corner of Wall Street and Broadway in New York City. Upon unraveling a mysterious clue, he is led inside an old church where he finds a passageway to a hidden staircase and intricate dumbwaiter system.

After some humorous interaction with his rivals who are out to steal the treasure, Gates finally realizes that a clue he gained early in the movie is the key to another secret passageway. Upon entering through this passageway he, and the others with him, realize that they have indeed found the treasure room. But it is dark, so they can see only a portion—until an old intricate system of oil lanterns is lit and the large room is illuminated, revealing the enormous treasure. It is the most significant historical treasure ever discovered...and the Gates family name is vindicated.

But it is still just another movie.

We have in store for us the greatest treasure of all time in the coming kingdom of Christ. The mysteries revealed shed further light on that kingdom and the events leading up to it.

Understanding is the means to great treasure.

Sometimes it's a changed vantage point that helps us see differently than before.

In giving these parables their due, we must distinguish between the interpretation and the application. The interpretation is one thing, while the application may vary slightly depending on timing and circumstance. The application would have been made by the disciples, it must be made by us, and it will in the future be made by those living during the Tribulation.

The application of these parables was necessary before the church began and will be necessary after the church is gone. The mysteries of the kingdom, therefore, are not the church; yet the application of the principles can and should be applied by the church.

All of these parables are about the kingdom of God and the preparatory work that leads up to it. The interpretation and application is good for every age until Jesus comes back in triumph.

We should, therefore, find great meaning in these passages without changing the intended meaning. The more good soil that receives the word of the kingdom; the more wheat produced; the larger the mustard tree grows; the more His children are willing to make the necessary sacrifices; the more God will be able to use us for His own glory and "provoke them to jealousy"![64]

The Jews today are still looking for and awaiting the coming kingdom of Messiah. They need to understand the mysteries of the kingdom. Our job is to apply what we learn so they might connect the dots. These mysteries give us greater insight and understanding as to what God is doing now and the certainty of what awaits us; interpreting them correctly is our chance at vindicating the name of God in regards to His kingdom.

NOTES

1 See Matthew 13:17.

2 Virkler, *Hermeneutics,* 163.

3 Ibid., 172.

4 See Matthew 13:10; Mark 4:1–12; Luke 8:4–10.

5 See Matthew 13:10–15.

6 The verb *granted* is a perfect passive participle, which describes an action completed in the past time with ongoing effects in the present; the verb *to know* is an aorist active infinitive, which defines the purpose of the previous verb.

7 See Matthew 13:11.

8 See Matthew 13:36.

9 Matthew 13:11.

10 John Nolland, *The Gospel of Matthew: A Commentary on the Greek Text* (Grand Rapids, MI: Wm. B. Eerdmans Publishing Company, 2005), 533.

11 Matthew 13:11, emphasis mine.

12 McClain, *The Greatness of the Kingdom*, 19.

13 Nolland, *The Gospel of Matthew,* 537.

14 See Matthew 13:39–40, 49.

15 See Matthew 18:1; 20:20–21.

16 See Luke 19:11.

17 See Acts 1:6.

18 See Matthew 13:17.

19 See Matthew 13:30, 39–40, 48.

20 See Matthew 16:18.

21 See Acts 2.

22 See Ephesians 2:11–3:13.

23 Ephesians 3:6.

24 Matthew 13:1–9, 18–23.

25 Matthew 13:19.

26 See Matthew 13:18–23.

27 Matthew 13:19.

28 Ibid.

29 Luke 8:12.

30 Luke 8:10.

31 Matthew 13:22.

32 Nolland, *The Gospel of Matthew,* 541.

33 See Matthew 13:9.

34 See Zechariah 9:9; Isaiah 11–12.

35 See Zechariah 12:10–13:7; Isaiah 59:20–21.

36 See Matthew 28:18–20.

37 Matthew 13:24–30, 36–43.

38 Matthew 13:36–43.

39 "What does it mean that Jesus is the Son of Man?" Gotquestions.org, accessed

March 7, 2011, http://www.gotquestions.org/Jesus-Son-of-Man.html.
40 See Matthew 13:38.
41 See Matthew 8:12.
42 See Matthew 13:43.
43 Matthew 13:26.
44 See Isaiah 43:21; Psalm 102:18–22.
45 Hebrews 1:3, 13.
46 Matthew 28:18–20.
47 Revelation 20:2–3.
48 Matthew 13:39–42.
49 Matthew 13:43.
50 Ibid.
51 Matthew 13:31–32.
52 See Daniel 2:44–45; 7:13–14, 22.
53 Nolland, *The Gospel of Matthew,* 552.
54 1 Thessalonians 4:17.
55 See Matthew 13:33.
56 Ibid.
57 See Matthew 13:44.
58 See Matthew 6:19, 33; 19:21.
59 See Matthew 13:45–46.
60 See Matthew 6:33.
61 See Matthew 13:47–50.
62 Matthew 13:49.
63 See Matthew 13:52.
64 Romans 11:11, NKJV.

TWELVE

WORTH
EVERYTHING

*Oh, the irony of knowing that one's
future happiness is dependent upon
the tragedies of one's past.*

Anonymous

Long-distance travel is difficult for an impatient person who
likes his personal space. I admit that I am not the most long-
suffering traveler—I want to get wherever I am going as quickly
as possible. My wife, Angie, would attest to the fact. I am not too
crazy about traffic, or about some civil engineer's layout for certain
cities. And I don't much care for airports, rental car hubs, hotels, or
trams.

I used to travel a lot for business before being in full-time
ministry. I was single, and the travel was lonely and frustrating.
Business travel is not at all like traveling for vacation somewhere
exotic, nor near as fun. Business travel is oftentimes hurried due
to the brevity of the trip, renting a car, navigating new territory,

meetings, meals, hotels, returning the rental car, getting to the airport, and always hurrying to catch the early flight home.

But the worst is being away all week, sleeping in an uncomfortable hotel bed, all that hustle and bustle to make the flight, drop off the rental car, ride the shuttle to the airport, make a mad dash into the airport, and then hastily glancing at the departure screen to find the flight number and destination, only to see that dreaded notice: *CANCELLED*.

In moments like these, it is impossible to conceal your disappointment. It is hard to find the good when plans for which you hoped, desired, and worked hard for are *CANCELLED*. Cancelled is just a frustrating concept: cancelled golf match due to weather; cancelled wedding due to cold feet, etc., etc...

As it pertains to the kingdom, there are large groups of people today who truly believe that because the nation of Israel rejected the kingdom Jesus offered them in His first coming, the promises of the kingdom have been CANCELLED. Even if some might not use the word *cancelled,* they imply the same thing by saying that the promises are being spiritually fulfilled in the church today. Either way, they seem to say, if the promises for a literal kingdom—the kingdom Jesus offered the nation—are not going to be fulfilled, then for all practical purposes they have been cancelled.

But wait a minute...that idea may not hold water. Let's take a look.

REJECTED BUT NOT DETERRED

Jesus entered the city of Jerusalem on what would be His last week on earth before He was put to death. Being truly heartbroken over Israel's rejection, He shed tears for the city as He looked down upon it from the Mount of Olives. As He wept, He said, "If you had known in this day, even you, the things which make for peace! But now they have been hidden from your eyes."[1] The day was a very significant day because it was foretold by Daniel the prophet as the time when the "Messiah shall be cut off."[2]

This last week of Jesus' life constituted Israel's day of visitation and the day that He, the Messiah, would be cut off. This day was so exact, being ordained by divine prophecy, that they could have calculated it. This day was exactly 483 years after the decree to rebuild Jerusalem in 444 BC, as Daniel prophesied. The rejection that had been prophesied was now being realized. But even Daniel, hundreds of years prior, also foresaw that this rejection did not eliminate the Messianic hope that would eventually come after the seventieth week.[3]

And of course Jesus knew the pain Israel was inflicting upon herself. Israel could have had the kingdom right then, but instead she would have to wait thousands of years and experience much hardship before she would have that opportunity again. God's promise to Israel would be fulfilled and she would still be offered the kingdom, for the promise was not dependent upon Israel's character, but on God's.

The rejection of Jesus by the nation of Israel did not mean that Jesus permanently withdrew the offer or that He *cancelled* the kingdom altogether. Instead, what it meant was that God would open the offer of the kingdom up to the Gentiles, causing Israel to become jealous and see her mistake. The kingdom was not cancelled, but delayed; and she would have another chance to serve Him as king.

> *The kingdom was not cancelled, but delayed.*

THE KINGDOM IS WHY JESUS CAME

There is no debate that Jesus came specifically to the nation of Israel with the offer of setting up their promised kingdom. When a Canaanite woman sought mercy from Jesus, He told her that He "was sent only to the lost sheep of the house of Israel."[4] When Jesus sent out the Twelve, He instructed them: "Do not go in the way of Gentiles, and do not enter any city of the Samaritans; but rather go to the lost sheep of the house of Israel."[5]

This specific message was to tender a genuine offer of the promised Messianic kingdom; and the target audience, the nation to whom these promises were given, was the chosen nation of Israel.

Jesus' public ministry centered on "proclaiming the gospel of the kingdom, and healing every kind of disease and every kind of sickness."[6] He sent out the twelve disciples and gave them the power to work miracles in order to validate the message He gave them to preach. They were to proclaim: "The kingdom of heaven is at hand."[7]

For the most part, this message and these miracles fell on blind eyes, deaf ears, and hard hearts; and they did not provoke the nation to respond positively.[8] Due to their poor response, Jesus reproached the cities where He and the disciples had ministered.[9]

The Light of the World was flooding the landscape, but they were blinded by their own selfish interests.

From a very early point in Jesus' ministry, the national rejection began to take substantive form as the Pharisees began seeking to destroy Him,[10] accusing Him of casting out demons by the power of Satan.[11] The signs and attesting miracles evidenced His Messianic authority, and yet they rejected Him anyway.

And though He was rejected in His own hometown of Nazareth,[12] He remained steadfast in His purpose of making His offer to the nation. In light of the mounting rejection, Jesus set His face toward Jerusalem to undergo the ultimate rejection of death that He knew awaited Him there.[13]

Before entering into Jerusalem, Jesus had been declaring that the kingdom was near. After this point, that message of imminence is absent. Jesus continued to unfold God's plan of the kingdom, but now He did it in light of His approaching rejection and the kingdom's postponement. As He traveled toward Jerusalem, He began preparing the disciples for the severity of the nation's rejection and His own death.[14] And He told His disciples many parables that reinforced the coming rejection and the consequent delay of the kingdom.

PARABLE OF DELAY

One of the most obvious parables of kingdom delay is recorded by Luke: the parable of the minas.[15] While enduring mounting, unofficial rejection from the religious leaders as He was nearing Jerusalem for the last time, Jesus knew that the disciples were thinking that the kingdom was going to appear immediately. He told them this parable to dispel that idea. The parable of the minas was His way of illustrating the rejection of the King and the *delay* of the kingdom until the King returned a second time.[16] This is obvious by His saying, "A nobleman went to a distant country to receive a kingdom...and then return."[17]

The parable also "delineates the role of a disciple in the time between the Lord's departure and His return."[18] This is seen in the nobleman's entrusting of stewardship to "ten of his slaves...and [saying] to them, 'Do business with this until I come back.'"[19] Upon his return and "after receiving the kingdom,"[20] the nobleman calls his servants together to evaluate their efforts in his absence. This parable clearly teaches, then, that the literal fulfillment of the kingdom is still an appropriate expectation. In no way is it implied that the kingdom has been cancelled. As Jesus specially indicated in Luke 19:11–12, it has only been *DELAYED*.

This event was before the Cross...the ultimate rejection to come.

AFTER THE CROSS

After the ultimate and definitive rejection of Jesus at the cross, and His resurrection three days later, Jesus appeared to many for forty days and taught on the "kingdom of God."[21] There is no reason to think that the meaning of *kingdom* had changed, or that the expectation and hope had been abolished or somehow vaporized. So we should assume that the kingdom had not been cancelled, nor had it suddenly become either an analogy or a "spiritual kingdom." Why would something that was totally real suddenly become something mystical or ethereal? And what would make us think that God would undo a promise He had made?

After Jesus "[appeared] to them over a period of forty days, and [spoke] of the things concerning the kingdom," the disciples inquired about the timing of the coming of the kingdom for Israel, not whether or not the kingdom was going to come.[22] The response of Jesus clearly indicates that the kingdom is still a future expectation. While He is not willing to give the exact time of His coming to set up the kingdom, He does indicate that the time is "fixed"[23] by the Father (in the same way that rewards are "prepared" in Matthew 20:23).

There is nothing in the teaching of Jesus, either before the cross or after, that gives any indication that the kingdom had been cancelled or that the promises of the kingdom would now be spiritually fulfilled in the church.

The kingdom is God's program which He ordained "from the foundation of the world."[24] He has made unilateral and guaranteed covenants to Israel that assure its fulfillment. It will certainly come to pass in exactly the manner promised. In addition, in the face of the rejection, Jesus and all those associated with Him maintained an expectation of a literal fulfillment of the kingdom promises, albeit after a delay.

But what about after the day of Pentecost...the birth of the church?

PAUL'S INFURIATING MESSAGE

The book of Acts tells us a great deal about the life of Paul. And what we see in Paul's life is crucial as we link the Gospels and the rest of the New Testament with what we've learned about the kingdom of Messiah.

As the book of Acts closes, we see the church in Jerusalem turn against Paul. The reason was not because Gentiles were coming to faith in Christ, because actually they "glorified God"[25] for this; rather, it was because Paul was teaching "against the nation, and against the Law, and against the temple." [26]Later, Paul would tell the church at Ephesus that the reason he was put in prison in Rome was "for the sake of you Gentiles."[27]

So what was Paul teaching that was against the nation, etc.? If it wasn't that salvation was being offered to the Gentiles through Christ, then what was it that angered them so?

Ephesians 3:6 says, "To be specific, that the Gentiles are fellow heirs and fellow members of the body, and fellow partakers of the promise in Christ Jesus through the gospel." Remember what the "gospel" was that Jesus was sharing? It was the message of the kingdom! (From the chapter called "Kingdom Within Grasp.")

This fact—that Paul was arrested for preaching that Gentiles shared in *the coming hope of Messiah*—is clearly revealed in the closing section of Acts. It started when Paul was in Jerusalem, after he had been seized and drug out of the temple. The people there were "seeking to kill him,"[28] but before they could do that a Roman commander ordered that Paul be bound in chains and locked in the barracks. Prior to entering the barracks, Paul obtained permission to address the angry, hostile crowd.

In his defense to the crowd[29] (the first of many defenses he gave), Paul recalled his upbringing and experience as a persecutor of the church and then the commission he received from Jesus on the road to Damascus. Yet the part of this defense that caused such a reaction from the Jewish Christians was when Paul told them that while he was in the temple in Jerusalem after his return from Damascus, Jesus appeared to Him again and said,

> "Make haste, and get out of Jerusalem quickly, because they will not accept your testimony about Me.... Go! For I will send you far away to the Gentiles."[30]

While the crowd listened to his entire defense, it was at this statement they wished him dead.[31] What angered the crowd to such a degree was not merely that Paul had been commissioned to preach to Gentiles; it was his alluding to the idea that Jesus was saying that Jews would not receive the testimony about Him. The implication to the crowd was that this was the reason Paul was teaching that the Law had been abolished and the hope of Israel was now available to the Gentiles. The *Bible Knowledge Commentary* picks up on exactly this point:

> Preaching to the Gentiles could not have caused such a response because the religious authorities of Israel had preached to Gentiles.... Paul's message that infuriated the mob was that Jews and Gentiles were equal without the Law of Moses."[32]

The equality Paul was teaching was not simply the "abolishment of the law," but also making Gentiles "fellow heirs...and fellow partakers of the promise in Christ Jesus."[33] This can be seen even more clearly in Paul's subsequent series of defenses.

On the very next day, the Roman commander ordered the chief priests and the Sanhedrin to assemble to hear Paul's defense. This is Paul's second defense of his ministry and message. In his opening, Paul said to the council that he was "on trial for the hope and resurrection of the dead!"[34] The hope is of the coming Messianic kingdom, which necessitates the resurrection of the dead so that those to whom the promises were made could inherit the hope attached to those promises.

THE PLOT THICKENS

When the hostility increased, Paul was transferred to a prison in Caesarea where he remained for two years. After an appeal to Caesar, Paul was interrogated by King Agrippa, who hoped to solidify the charge against Paul so that something could be written and sent with Paul to Rome.[35] In his defense, Paul tells King Agrippa,

"Now I am standing trial for the hope of the promise made by God to our fathers; the promise to which our twelve tribes hope to attain."[36]

Here the issue becomes very clear. Paul is imprisoned for the promise God made to the fathers of the nation of Israel. The hope of that promise was given originally to Abraham and later to David that guaranteed a land, the land of promise, and a seed to rule over the dynasty of David. That is the hope of Israel. Dr. J. Dwight Pentecost comments on this hope:

> The prophets of the Old Testament had proclaimed a message of hope that caused Israel to eagerly anticipate the fulfillment of God's covenants and promises to them. David's son the Messiah would come to bring peace, righteousness, and prosperity to the nation. He would come as Savior to redeem and Sovereign to reign. The nations which had persecuted Israel would be subjugated to Him, and Israel would know the promised peace which the Prince of Peace would bring. Her accumulated sins would be put away and she would experience forgiveness and life in righteousness. Such was the hope of Israel.[37]

The reason Paul was on trial was because he was preaching that Gentiles now shared in that hope; this is what angered the crowd in Jerusalem. This hope that Paul was imprisoned for was the hope of the literal fulfillment of God's promises to be realized in a literal Messianic age upon this earth.

Let's stop a moment and look at what this means and how these pieces fit together:

- *To whom are the promises of a kingdom given?*

  Answer: They were given to Abraham, David, and the twelve tribes of Israel.

- *What is the hope of Israel?*

  Answer: The kingdom and a king to rule.

- *What new message did Paul proclaim (which angered the Jews)?*

  Answer: That the law was abolished and Gentiles were equal with the Jews and therefore could share in the "hope of Israel"—the kingdom was now being offered to Jews and Gentiles alike.

- *What was the condition which must be met?*

  Answer: Repentance and good deeds.

As Paul continued his defense to King Agrippa, he recounts his conversion and commission received directly from Jesus: "to open their eyes so that they may turn from darkness to light and from the dominion of Satan to God, that they may receive forgiveness of sins and an inheritance among those who have been sanctified by faith in Me."[38] Paul then summarizes that commission in his defense to King Agrippa:

> "I did not prove disobedient to the heavenly vision, but kept declaring to those of Damascus...Jerusalem... the region of Judea, and even to the Gentiles, that they should repent and turn to God, performing deeds appropriate to repentance."[39]

Paul explained that this was the reason he was seized in the temple and why some attempted to put him to death.[40] That this message is quite similar to those of John the Baptist and Jesus in their proclamations of the kingdom should not be overlooked. Paul was not only teaching eternal salvation by faith alone in Christ alone; he was teaching the kingdom as reward to those who would repent and "[perform] deeds appropriate to repentance."[41]

And then Paul offers King Agrippa this telling statement:

> "Having obtained help from God, I stand to this day testifying both to small and great, stating nothing but what the Prophets and Moses said was going to take place; that the Christ was to suffer, and that by reason of His resurrection from the dead He would be the first to proclaim light both to the Jewish people and to the Gentiles."[42]

Paul was not merely focusing upon the gospel of salvation by grace through faith apart from works. His ministry and message were much broader than that and involved "repentance and good deeds." Paul's message was about the future coming, literal reign of Messiah; the hope of Israel. The fact that Paul was not teaching a mystery form of a spiritual kingdom should be obvious, for if he had been, the Jews would have no reason for their animosity.

Paul fully understood that the kingdom was not cancelled!

A FINAL DEFENSE

When Paul finally reached Rome and stood before the

prominent Jews, he defended himself yet one more time and said, "I am wearing this chain for the sake of the hope of Israel."[43]

A few days later his defense continued in a more formal setting. Luke records that Paul "was explaining to them by solemnly testifying about the kingdom of God and trying to persuade them concerning Jesus, from both the Law of Moses and from the Prophets, from morning until evening."[44] Once again, another comment from the *Bible Knowledge Commentary*:

> The hope of Israel was more than a resurrection; it meant fulfillment of the Old Testament promises to Israel...the term "kingdom of God" includes the death and resurrection of Christ as its basis but also looks ahead to Christ's reign on earth. It is clearly eschatological in significance.[45]

Luke summarizes Paul's time, and closes the book of Acts, with this description of Paul's ministry during his two-year house arrest in Rome:

> And he stayed two full years in his own rented quarters, and was welcoming all who came to him, preaching the kingdom of God and teaching concerning the Lord Jesus Christ with all openness, unhindered.[46]

Paul went to prison over the message given him by Jesus about the right of Gentiles to share in the coming Messianic kingdom. For a person of Paul's intelligence to go to prison for a cause he was deeply convinced of, implies that he thought the kingdom was still a future hope. Paul's message throughout the book of Acts was that

Gentiles had the opportunity to be fellow heirs and fellow partakers with Israel in the inheritance of the coming Messianic kingdom.

Even though he taught that Gentiles share in the hope of Israel, Paul never wavered from believing in the national blessing for Israel. He delineates clearly these beliefs in his letter to the Romans.[47] Despite the fact that the church, which is composed of Jew and Gentile, shares in the promise of the kingdom, it in no way insinuates that God had forsaken His people or changed, cancelled, or revoked His covenants to them as His chosen people.[48]

ISRAEL: GOD'S CHOSEN PEOPLE

Paul tells the church at Rome that Israel's rejection did not at all mean that God was rejecting His people.[49] God has a future for the nation of Israel, but their stumbling has brought Messianic salvation to Gentiles.[50] And the reason given for this taking place is "to make them jealous."[51]

The "partial hardening"[52] of Israel was for our benefit, but that hardening will only last until the end of this age. Then Israel will experience the deliverance God has always promised.[53] The reason that God must fulfill His promise to the nation is that the "gifts and the calling of God are irrevocable."[54] Because God gave the promises to the nation of Israel, He must fulfill those promises to that chosen nation.

The book of Revelation makes it clear that the outpouring of salvation during the Tribulation will be significantly upon the Jews, for it is through the great and awesome day of the Lord that God purges that nation, creating a righteous remnant. Paul said, "Now if their transgression is riches for the world and their failure is riches for the Gentiles, how much more will their fulfillment be!"[55]

Their kingdom is coming. It has only been delayed...but it is still ON!

OH, THE IRONY...

God has not yet fulfilled His promise to Israel because they have yet to meet the condition God gave them for the kingdom's establishment. The offer of the kingdom to that chosen nation was withdrawn, yet will be offered again. There will be a time when Israel meets the condition that God has set, and God will fulfill all that He has promised. Unlike any of us, God cannot lie,[56] and His word will not return to Him void without accomplishing all that He intends.[57]

> *Their rejection is our gain.*

We are being blessed with mercy and grace now because of Israel's rejection of Jesus, and we have the privilege of sharing in the inheritance of the coming kingdom. This is great news for us.

Israel's rejection of Christ paved a way for you and me to share in the coming kingdom. Their rejection is our gain, but only because the kingdom has been delayed, not cancelled. The promises will be realized in the literal reign of Messiah upon this earth, and all those who have persevered to the end will return with Jesus to reign with Him.

When a flight is cancelled it is hard to find the good; but if it is only delayed, it can be beneficial in a number of ways. If, for example, you were late arriving at the airport, a delayed flight saves you from missing the flight. It may also be an avenue for other travelers to join your flight. It may also be an opportunity for greater blessing. In years past, it was regularly the case that if your flight was delayed the airline would offer a free meal, or if you were lucky, a travel voucher, or the greatest benefit of all, an upgrade to first class.

"Oh, the irony of knowing that one's future happiness is dependent upon the tragedies of one's past." Our future happiness as Gentiles is fully dependent upon Israel's having rejected Jesus, our Savior. Through her refusal to see Him for who He is, God's future glory will be displayed exponentially more brightly as Gentiles are added to the kingdom. When the kingdom promises are fulfilled to the nation of Israel, we too will share in that glory.

NOTES

1 Luke 19:42.
2 Daniel 9:26.
3 See Daniel 9:24–25.
4 Matthew 15:24.
5 Matthew 10:5–6.
6 Matthew 9:35.
7 Matthew 10:7.
8 Matthew 13:13–15
9 See Matthew 11:20.
10 See Matthew 12:14.
11 See Matthew 12:24.
12 Matthew 13:53–58.
13 Matthew 16:21.
14 Matthew 20:17–19.
15 See Luke 19:11–27.
16 Ibid.
17 Luke 19:12.
18 D. A. Carson, Walter Wessel, and Walter L. Liefeld, *Matthew, Mark, Luke: The Expositor's Bible Commentary,* ed. Frank Gaebelein (Grand Rapids, MI: Zondervan, 1984), 1008.
19 Luke 19:13.
20 Luke 19:15.
21 Acts 1:3.
22 See Acts 1:6.
23 Acts 1:7.
24 Matthew 25:34.
25 Acts 11:18.
26 Acts 21:21 and 28
27 Ephesians 31.
28 Acts 21:31.
29 See Acts 22:1–21.
30 Acts 22:18, 21
31 See Acts 22:22.
32 Walvoord, *Bible Knowledge Commentary*, 418.
33 Ephesians 3:6.
34 Acts 23:6; again in Acts 24:14–15, 21.
35 See Acts 25:23–27.
36 Acts 26:6–7.
37 Thomas Ice, *When the Trumpet Sounds: Today's Foremost Authorities Speak Out on End-Time Controversy*, ed. Timothy Demy (Eugene, OR: Harvest House Publishers, 1995), 166.
38 Acts 26:18.

39 Acts 26:19–20.
40 See Acts 26:21.
41 Acts 26:20b.
42 Acts 26:22–23.
43 Acts 28:20.
44 Acts 28:23.
45 Walvoord, *Bible Knowledge Commentary*, 430.
46 Acts 28:30–31.
47 See Romans 11:1–2.
48 See Romans 11:29.
49 See Romans 11:1–2.
50 See Romans 11:11.
51 Ibid.
52 Romans 11:25.
53 See Romans 11:26.
54 Romans 11:29.
55 Romans 11:12.
56 See Numbers 23:19.
57 See Isaiah 55:11.

THIRTEEN

WELCOME TO THE FAMILY

Every good thing bestowed and every perfect gift is from above

James 1:17

I was ashamed...I did not want anyone to find out...I didn't want anyone to know that I was adopted.

Those are the words of the late founder of Wendy's, Dave Thomas, when he first found out he was an adopted child. Dave was born July 2, 1932, to a single mother and adopted six weeks later. Even though his adopted family life was anything but perfect, Dave realized that it was better than the alternatives of an orphanage or foster care, because at least his adoptive father was a good provider.

No wonder Dave Thomas became such an advocate for adoption.

In fact, in 1990 President George Bush asked Dave to be the

national spokesperson for Adoption Works...for Everyone initiative. And in 1992 Dave established the very successful Dave Thomas Foundation for Adoption, which continues to this day. Adoption made a profound difference in the life of Dave Thomas, despite his feelings of shame and rejection. The opportunities afforded Dave, and so many others like him, would not have been available had he not been adopted. Adoption was a life changer.

Adoption in our contemporary understanding is a process, defined by Webster as "to take into one's family legally."[1] This is *not* the same idea as the "adoption as sons" referred to in the Bible. The biblical idea focuses on the state, not the process. Let me explain.

This is good stuff. No, this is great stuff!

Diving deeper into this matter means pulling out our study tools such as a Greek dictionary or expository dictionary (well, mine, at least) and our logical, step-by-step hermeneutical (i.e., the art and science of interpretation) method.

WHAT DOES THE WORD ADOPTION MEAN?

The word that is translated as "adoption as sons" is the Greek word "*huiothesia*."[2] This is a compound word containing the word *son* (Greek: *huios*) and the word to *put, place, set* (from Greek: *tithemi*). This latter word can indicate placement or appointment. The idea in the compound word (*huiothesia*), then, is *son placement, sonship, son standing, son appointment*. This term indicates what a son is appointed to/for a situation.

Fairly painless so far, right?

What is important to realize is that this word does *not* describe the process of taking orphans, or unnatural children, and making them a part of a new family.

Instead, the word simply indicates what is available to the child in the new state that he is in. Or, as *Vine's Expositors Dictionary* states, *huiothesia* "signifies the place and condition of a son...the dignity of the relationship of believers as sons; it is not a putting into the family by spiritual birth, but a putting into the position of sons."[3]

We "become children of God" by receiving Jesus Christ by faith alone,[4] or as Paul states, "you are all sons of God through faith in Christ Jesus."[5] This is the legal process, but it is called justification, not adoption.

So the "adoption as sons" in the Bible refers to our state and status; to what is available to us as children of God. Harold Hoehner in his commentary on Ephesians draws out this distinction when he states that the sonship "refers to what the saint has been predestined to...or [his] appointment."[6] In other words, adoption is something that is available to one who is a saint. And later Hoehner adds that this appointment was "to continue the family line and maintain property ownership. This son became the patria potestas ('power of the father') in the next generation."[7]

> *Adoption is the appointment and the privileges.*

The word *adoption* may be the word that confuses us, but it is not altogether incorrect. Adoption as sons is the appointment and the privileges that sons (or daughters) have. It is what is true of one who is a son, or in our case, one who has become a son by faith.

THE TIMING

As we have seen, our son status has to do with certain rights and privileges that are available to us. But when do we realize those rights? When do we benefit from those privileges?

Paul indicates that while we have presently received a "spirit of adoption,"[8] the actual fulfillment of the adoption is something we "[await] eagerly."[9] This seems to indicate that the timing of our full realization of our rights and privileges is yet future.

I would maintain that those rights and privileges will be realized in the glory of the coming kingdom. The kingdom is when we get our inheritance. These are the material riches of the Father and Christ Jesus.

The inquisitive reader may ask at this point, "Why was such an offer of adoption even given?" How astute of you to inquire! And the story behind the answer is one we all know. The story is of promise, praise, rejection, betrayal, sorrow, death, resurrection, mystery, and hope. It is the story of the Messiah.

These rights and riches that are ours by nature of our sonship, our inheritance, are all related to the promised kingdom. These privileges and riches were originally promised and given to the nation of Israel and therefore belong to Israel,[10] but we have now been made "fellow heirs...and fellow partakers of the promise in Christ Jesus."[11] In light of the rejection by the nation of Israel, Jesus postponed the kingdom and in so doing opened up the blessings and privileges of that kingdom to a much larger audience; He offered them to Gentiles who by faith become "heirs according to promise."[12]

Since the covenants and promises of the coming kingdom are all possessed and enjoyed by the family of God, the only way for us to partake of them is to be brought into that family. That is what Paul means when he said, "If you belong to Christ, then you are Abraham's descendants, heirs according to promise."[13] We had to in some way be connected to Abraham since the Messiah and His kingdom was promised to him and all other promises were given to his seed.

The firstborn sons, the nation of Israel, because of their rejection of Christ at His first coming, have been temporarily set aside as a nation. Consequently, an invitation has been sent out to every individual who will come (whether Jew or Gentile). In this way, Gentiles are given the opportunity to inherit roles or realms of rulership within the kingdom as adopted sons.

What an amazing story and benevolent turn of events.

The remarkable grace and generosity of which cannot be overlooked.

Even Jesus Himself spoke about the offer of adoption which would be given to the Gentiles.

EARLY INDICATION OF INHERITANCE SHARED

Jesus gave a foreshadowing of this opportunity for Gentiles to share in the kingdom promises. We see a picture of this early on in His teaching when He encountered a Gentile man, a centurion, who sought Jesus to heal his sick servant. The interaction between the centurion and Jesus reveals this Gentile's remarkable faith in Christ, which, in turn, elicits a powerful response from Jesus: "I have not found such great faith with anyone in Israel."[14]

That is a remarkable statement, considering the historical setting and time.

As a result of seeing this great faith in action, Jesus said something to this Gentile that ought to catch our attention: "I say to you that many will come from east and west, and recline at the table with Abraham, Isaac and Jacob in the kingdom of heaven; but the sons of the kingdom will be cast out."[15]

Now that is another statement that should catch our attention. A double whammy!

Not only is an indication given here that Jesus foresaw that many from the nation of Israel, the sons of the kingdom, would forfeit their right to share in the coming kingdom; it also indicates that Gentiles, represented by this centurion because of his faithfulness, were going to earn the right to partake in the kingdom promised to Israel. That's downright prophetic!

While in the temple in Jerusalem, Jesus told another parable about the kingdom. In this one He compares the kingdom to a wedding feast. The wedding feast is not attended by the initial invitees, who proved unworthy to join in the celebration. As a result, the invitation goes out to a much wider audience, and the hall is filled by those who respond to this second invitation. Interestingly enough, these include "both evil and good"[16] individuals.

The first group invited to the wedding feast is a reference to the nation of Israel, to whom Jesus initially offered the kingdom. The second wave of invitees includes everyone, irrespective of their nationality. The invitation is to share in the wedding feast of the King's son; the feast is a metaphor for the kingdom promised to Israel in the Old Testament and offered by Jesus in the New Testament.

And just to be clear, the invitation is not for eternal salvation.[17] Jesus was teaching that the invitation to the promised kingdom, the wedding feast given by the King for his son, would be extended beyond the chosen nation to "whom belongs the adoption as sons, and the glory and the covenants and the giving of the Law and the temple service and the promises."[18]

Not only did Jesus, on more than one occasion, talk about this new idea of believing Gentiles becoming heirs to the kingdom, but another standout in the Bible, Paul, proclaimed the same message. In fact, it was for this message that he was imprisoned and plots to kill him were hatched.

INDICATED BY PAUL

Paul was a Jew, a Roman citizen, an educated man,[19] a son of a Pharisee, and a Pharisee himself,[20] and because of his religious training, he was an expert in the Old Testament Scriptures, the Law, the oral traditions, and the hope of Israel.[21] The hope of Israel is the prize for which everyone must strive. Listen to what Paul says about his own pursuit of this prize:

> Not that I have already obtained it or have already become perfect, but I press on so that I may lay hold of that for which also I was laid hold of by Christ Jesus. Brethren, I do not regard myself as having laid hold of it yet; but one thing I do: forgetting what lies behind and reaching forward to what lies ahead, I press on toward the goal for the prize of the upward call of God in Christ Jesus.[22]

The prize? What prize could Paul have not yet attained? What prize must Paul wait for until the "upward call"? If anyone had it all, it would have been Paul.

The prize Paul was pressing forward to lay hold of is Israel's certain hope of the kingdom age of Messiah; it is what the "twelve tribes hope to attain"[23] and what Paul endured so many trials and hardships to attain.

Paul explains in a number of places God's plan to incorporate other sons into the inheritance of the promised kingdom. In fact, Paul indicates that it is these promises that God has pre-appointed the church to share in.[24] Paul was commissioned by Jesus to preach to believing Gentiles that they had a right, by way of sonship, to share in the "hope of Israel."[25] In fact, Paul had agitated the Christians in Jerusalem and was imprisoned by countrymen for preaching this message.[26]

This was shocking to Jewish Christians in Jerusalem (who seemingly offered no support to Paul upon his arrest), the Jews from Asia, and to Paul's Jewish countrymen because this truth was never revealed in the Old Testament. It was a mystery.[27] The Jews

GOING DEEPER

There has been much debate as to the mystery that Paul spoke about in his letter to the Ephesians. Many have suggested that the church is the mystery of which Paul wrote. But the church is not the mystery per se (at least, not entirely); the mystery is also the kingdom benefit that comes to the church on account of its "son" status.

The mystery to which Paul initially referred was that which was "according to His kind intention which He purposed in Him with a view to an administration suitable to the fullness of the times, that is, the summing up of all things in Christ, things in the heavens and things on the earth."[28]

Let's consult an expert to guide us here.

Harold W. Hoehner in his commentary on Ephesians states that "the present verse speaks...more particularly to a final stage...the time yet future when God is going to unite all of creation under Christ's headship in the fullness of time, the eschatological age of Messiah's rule."[29] Well, that can only be the timing of His coming kingdom, because only then will all things be subjected to Him!

This is confirmed in Psalm 110, where we read:

The LORD says to my lord: Sit at my right hand until I make your enemies a footstool for your feet." The LORD will extend your mighty scepter from Zion, saying, "Rule in the midst of your enemies. Your troops will be willing on your day of battle. Arrayed in holy splendor.[30]

Interestingly enough, Jesus connected this very passage to His Messianic authority as the Son of God.[31]

thought that the golden age to come was only for them since they had endured so much for their connection to the one true God.

MYSTERY IN EPHESIANS

When Paul elaborates on the mystery just two chapters later (following his first reference), he sheds further light on the subject by saying, "The Gentiles are fellow heirs and fellow members of the body, and fellow partakers of the promise in Christ Jesus through the gospel."[32] That sounds pretty clear! The mystery is that Gentiles, because of their son status, get to share in the inheritance of the coming kingdom. As a Gentile myself, I say: Praise God!

While gentiles were formerly:

"separate from Christ,

excluded from the commonwealth of Israel,

and strangers to the covenants of promise;"[33]

they have now been made:

"fellow heirs,

and fellow members of the body,

and fellow partakers of the promise in Christ Jesus."[34]

Or as Paul told the church at Rome, Gentiles are:

"fellow heirs with Christ...that we may also be glorified with Him."[35]

Just as this message shocked the Jews of Paul's day, it might be equally shocking today since many believe that the church has no right to share in the promises of the coming kingdom since those promises "belong to Israel."

> *We have a right to share in His kingdom.*

While this is certainly a major tenet of a certain theological system, it seems to miss the point of Paul's teaching on the kingdom. Gentiles have sonship and are heirs (with Jews).

We have a right to share in His kingdom.

Paul taught that the church, consisting of believing Jew and Gentile in one spiritual universal body, is heir of something else, something that is directly related to the commonwealth of Israel and the covenants of promise; they are heirs and partakers of the coming kingdom.

This inheritance is addressed by Paul in Romans 8:12–30. There he wrote about the importance of the church living by the spirit and enduring suffering *for the sake of the hope of glory* as fellow heirs with Christ. Members of the church, the body of Christ, including believing Jew and Gentile alike, are fellow heirs with Christ in a coming glory. The glory Paul mentions in this section of Romans is not heaven; it is a reference to the coming kingdom of Messiah. The glory is our "hope;"[36] it is a future glory "[yet] to be revealed to us,"[37] one that involves the removal of the curse from the whole earth.[38] This hope, this glory centers upon this earth, not on some heavenly destiny.

The church's right to participate in that future, glorious kingdom—the establishment of which Jesus taught all believers to pray—led Paul to anticipate a question from the church at Rome: *Then what about Israel?*

A very natural and expected question according to the progression!

WHAT ABOUT ISRAEL?

Paul's answer is explained in Romans 9–11. There he clearly distinguishes the place of Israel and the place of the church: two separate and distinct entities joining together for service in that coming kingdom, but remaining distinct!

The faithful Israel will be involved in the earthly kingdom promised to them, covering the physical land mass that God gave them in the Abrahamic covenant. Ultimately, Jesus will be their

King, ruling from Jerusalem, but exercising a dominion that extends beyond Israel to the entire world. Nevertheless, Israel will have her *own* sovereign kingdom, completely independent of all Gentile influences. The apostles will be rewarded the right to reign over the twelve tribes of Israel during the millennial kingdom.[39]

At the same time, throughout Jesus' reign over all the rest of the earthly kingdoms, the faithful of the church will serve Him by reigning over the Gentile nations. This may be the place where America finds its role in the millennial reign of Christ.

It is obvious from the above explanation that Israel's place in the coming kingdom is not at all endangered by the church's involvement. But Paul wants to make this clear beyond all doubt in his discussion of these matters in Romans 9–11. As a result, he basically asked the following questions: *If the church is a fellow heir with Christ and may be glorified with Him,*[40] *then what about Israel? Is Israel forsaken of God?* Paul's answers are just as straightforward: God forbid![41]

Israel's rejection of Christ has not caused God to withdraw forever His promises to them, because "God has not rejected His people whom He foreknew."[42] Their "stumble"[43] did, however, lead to an inheritance being extended to all Gentiles who come by faith and persevere in faith (calling upon the name of the Lord).[44]

According to Paul, "their [Israel] transgression is riches for the world and their failure is riches for the Gentiles"[45] so that the Gentiles are now rich with an inheritance, a share, a partaking, in the coming blessings of the Messianic kingdom without usurping any of Israel's promised blessings and inheritance.

How awesome is that!

GENTILE SALVATION PROVOKES JEALOUSY

Adding to the intrigue in this saga of Gentiles being offered a share in the hope of Israel, Gentiles within the church are being used by God as instruments to make Israel jealous. Let's explore.

Paul said that "salvation has come to the Gentiles, to make them jealous."[46] This much is clear! (For further study of the concept of salvation referred to here, and in the whole book of Romans, see the Going Deeper section in the chapter's end.)

And what would make Israel jealous? It is not *only* the salvation which we have already realized in justification (salvation from sin's penalty). It is not *only* the salvation we are realizing presently in sanctification (salvation over sin's power). But it *is* a salvation which is "nearer to us than when we first believed"[47]: unmistakably, plainly, and undeniably a salvation in the future when Christ comes to set up His glorious kingdom.

The whole plan of salvation (in its entirety) is available to Gentiles to make the Jews jealous.[48]

Remember Paul's personal experience in Jerusalem? It explains this jealousy perfectly. The thing which led to his arrest was not that Jesus was saving Gentiles by grace through faith, but that He was teaching that the Law was abolished[49] and Gentiles, who were formerly "separate from Christ, excluded from the commonwealth of Israel, and strangers to the covenants of promise, having no hope and without God,"[50] but are now "fellow heirs...and fellow partakers of the promise in Christ Jesus."[51]

This is the way that a natural/firstborn son is made jealous of an adopted/younger son. When the adopted/younger son gains the privilege of participating in the natural/firstborn son's inheritance, the firstborn son becomes extremely jealous, especially if he temporarily lost his inheritance! This is the stuff of jealousy!

Gentiles, about whom it can now be said that there is no "distinction"[52] from firstborn sons, have gained access to "abounding riches" that will be realized in the coming age "for all who call on Him"[53] and "continue in His kindness."[54]

The distinction is set aside because Gentiles have been "grafted in" to the "rich root" "among them [Israel]" and "have become partakers with them [Israel)]" of the rich root which guarantees the Messianic blessing of earthly glory! [55]

But there is a catch! The only way for Gentiles to remain in the place of blessing is to "stand by [their] faith."[56] As Paul stated in the opening of his letter, "The righteous man shall live by faith."[57] The risk always remains that if they do not persevere in faith, they will be cut off from the blessings of the Messianic age. But regardless of what happens to the Gentiles, the nation of Israel will be grafted back into the rich root and "be saved"[58] (in the full sense of the word!) into the kingdom because the "gifts and the calling of God are irrevocable."[59]

Paul summarizes the whole section (Romans 9–11) by saying that "a partial hardening has happened to Israel until the fullness of the Gentiles has come in; so all Israel will be saved."[60] The salvation Paul has in mind is physical deliverance into the future Messianic kingdom. This understanding of the term *saved* is confirmed by Paul's quotation from Isaiah the prophet, when Isaiah foretold of a time when Messiah would come to set up His kingdom and deliver Israel.[61]

This partial hardening to the nation of Israel is seen as a good thing for any who will put their trust in Christ today and live for His glory. But that hardening has a time limit to it, for it will continue only *until* the end of the times of the Gentiles. At that time God will fulfill His promise to the nation of Israel of their glorious kingdom because the "gifts and the calling of God are irrevocable."[62] God must save Israel, delivering her into her glorious, future kingdom in the promised land upon this earth.

ENOUGH TO GO AROUND

My wife and I have two natural born sons; those boys belong to us regardless of what they do, or don't do. And my sons both have a birthright to anything that I leave behind as a part of my estate. That is their inheritance. If we chose to adopt another child, a little girl, we would be making that child a part of our family as well. The adoption in our day is the legal process; the result is that she has a right in all matters of the family.

As a part of our family she belongs. This is a fact that would never change, regardless of any issue or circumstance that may arise. As a part of our family she too becomes an heir to my estate.

If, however, any one of those three children decides to waste their lives and live in rebellion to me, their mother, or to God, I have the right and the responsibility to hold back their share of the inheritance. I will, however, never disown them or cease to love them.

This is similar to what the Bible teaches about how God deals with us as His children. He graciously saves us, and we are reconciled to Him and made a part of His family.[63] In so doing, He makes us heirs of a future inheritance which He wants to share with us.[64] Regardless of any issue or circumstance that may arise, He will never leave us or forsake us.[65] He may take away our inheritance, but God will never lose us. We will remain His sons forever!

If we could recognize the distinction between the free gift of God in eternal salvation and the inheritance that we now have a right to as fellow heirs, we would be well on our way of resolving great biblical dilemmas and living in the freedom we have for the glory of God. It will surely be worth it.

Welcome to the family...now live like a son and secure your inheritance.

GOING DEEPER

Salvation in Romans: The term salvation in the book of Romans is never used to refer to salvation from sin's penalty; Paul calls that justification (where Paul uses either the verb dikaioō or the nouns dikaiōsis or dikaiosunē). As one writer stated, "The term salvation or saved in Romans is not an equivalent to justification or regeneration (or redemption or reconciliation for that matter). It is broader than the matter of justification, but dependent upon the reality of justification" (Dr. B. Dale Taliaferro, unpublished notes on Romans). The salvation being discussed in Romans 9–11 is more than justification, so when we read that "with the mouth he confesses, resulting in salvation" or "whoever calls upon the name of the Lord will be saved," we must not conclude that these are conditions of justification (eternal salvation from sin's penalty...being declared righteous). The only condition for justification in Romans 10, as every other place in Scripture, is faith. This much is obvious when we see that "with the heart a person believes, resulting in righteousness (dikaiosunē)"(Romans 10:10a). Therefore, confessing Jesus as Lord or calling on Him is not a condition for eternal salvation/justification, but it is certainly a necessary condition of sanctification with a view toward glorification. It is an issue of following Christ; an issue of discipleship. Meeting the condition will result in the attainment of rewards that determines one's service in the glorious kingdom that is coming. This is similar to Jesus' instructions to His disciples about the need to "confess [Him] before men."[66] The disciple who obeys that command receives the promise from Jesus that He will "confess him before the Father."[67] The confession and calling upon the Lord will result in "abounding riches."[68] If the context means anything, then the abounding riches will be experienced in the coming glorious kingdom. This certainly suits Paul's quotation in Romans 10:13 of the prophecy from Joel 2:32, which historically was given as prophetic admonition for the coming day of the Lord when God would "restore the fortunes to Judah."[69]

Many people have mistakenly interpreted these passages, and others like them, to mean that grace alone though faith alone is insufficient for justification and that faith must be coupled with at least one act, confession. The failure in this view is not realizing that the salvation here is much broader than justification. This error is compounded by adding conditions (e.g., confession) to the free gift of salvation by grace alone through faith alone. The apostle Paul, writing under the inspiration of the Spirit of God, is adamant that justification is always by grace through faith apart from any works whatsoever.[70] If I have to choose between what others have said or are saying, and what Paul was clear on, I think I'll stick with Paul.

In Romans 10, one thing, faith, makes you a part of the team. The other, confession, is like coming to practice and working on your free throws. The two are not the same, although one is certainly dependent on the other.

For years these verses, specifically Romans 10:9, 13, have been used in an evangelistic gospel tract known as the "Romans' Road to Salvation." Upon maintaining the distinction between heaven/eternity and the coming kingdom, and between the three aspects of salvation—justification, sanctification, and glorification—these verses take on a whole new meaning and are easily harmonized with Paul's grace alone through faith alone salvation teachings.

I understand that since the salvation referred to in Romans 10 is not about getting to heaven, then the "Romans' Road to Salvation" needs to be rerouted. But this detour is one that no one wants to miss; it is a reroute to glory, one that is manifested upon the earth in fulfillment of all of God's promises and covenants! It is a detour that takes us to a paradise as it was originally intended by God. This is a route worth taking.

NOTES

1 Webster's II New College Dictionary (Houghton and Mifflin, 2001)

2 Romans 8:15, 23; 9:4, Galatians 4:5; Ephesians 1:5.

3 W. E. Vine, *Vine's Complete Expository Dictionary of Old and New Testament Words* (Nashville: Thomas Nelson Publishers, 1996), 13–14.

4 John 1:12.

5 Galatians 3:26.

6 Harold W. Hoehner, *Ephesians: An Exegetical Commentary* (Ada, MI: Baker Academic, 2002), 194.

7 Ibid., 196.

8 Romans 8:15.

9 Romans 8:23.

10 See Romans 9:4.

11 Ephesians 3:6.

12 Galatians 3:29.

13 Ibid.

14 Matthew 8:10.

15 Matthew 8:11–12.

16 Matthew 22:10.

17 This much is clear from the consequence of the man who responded to the invitation to the wedding feast, but was not himself prepared to join in the celebration. He was not "choice" because he had not dressed himself with faithfulness.

18 Romans 9:4.

19 Acts 22:3.

20 Acts 23:6; 26:5.

21 Acts 26:6–7; 28:20.

22 Philippians 3:12–14.

23 Acts 26:6–7.

24 See Romans 8:29–30; Ephesians 1:5, 11; 3:6.

25 Acts 28:20; see also 23:6; 26:6–7.

26 See Acts 20:23; Ephesians 3:1.

27 Ephesians 1:9–10; 3:1–6.

28 Ephesians 1:9–10.

29 Hoehner, *Ephesians*, 224.

30 Psalm 110:1–3a (NIV).

31 See Matthew 22:41–45.

32 Ephesians 3:6.

33 Ephesians 2:12.

34 Ephesians 3:6.

35 Romans 8:17.

36 Romans 5:2.

37 Romans 8:18.

38 See Romans 8:22–23.
39 See Matthew 19:28.
40 See Romans 8:17.
41 See Romans 11:1.
42 Romans 11:2.
43 Romans 11:11.
44 See Romans 10:10–13.
45 Romans 11:12.
46 Romans 11:11.
47 Romans 11:13.
48 In Greek it reads literally as "salvation to Gentiles."
49 See Ephesians 2:14–15.
50 Ephesians 2:12.
51 Ephesians 3:6.
52 Romans 10:12; Galatians 3:28.
53 Romans 10:12–13.
54 Romans 11:22.
55 Romans 11:17
56 Romans 11:20.
57 Romans 1:17.
58 Romans 11:26.
59 Romans 11: 29.
60 Romans 11:25–26.
61 See Romans 11:26–27; quoting Isaiah 59:20–21.
62 Romans 11:29.
63 See Romans 3:24; 8:17.
64 See Romans 8:17b; Ephesians 1;11; 3:6.
65 See Hebrews 13:5.
66 See Matthew 10:32; Luke 12:8.
67 See Matthew 10:32; Luke 12:8; Revelation 3:5.
68 See Romans 10:12b.
69 See Joel 3:1.
70 See Romans 3:28; 4:4–5; 14–16; Ephesians 2:8–9.

FOURTEEN

SWEET HARMONY

Harmony makes small things grow; lack of it makes great things decay.

Anonymous

Music is an agreeable harmony, said Johann Sebastian Bach. In music, harmony is the sound of two or more musical notes that are pleasing to the ear.

We've all heard it before. It can be wonderfully soothing or powerfully stirring. There's something intoxicating about singers or musicians performing in perfect harmony. You just want to sit and listen to it, lose yourself in the sound. Done well, simple harmony turns into something fluid and moving, emotive and sweet.

But the opposite is equally true: disharmony is irritating, agitating, and can bring a musical performance to a screeching halt.

Harmony in music is essential to enjoyment.

Harmony in theology is essential to abundant life.

Our term harmony is derived from the Greek term ἁρμονία (harmonia) which means joint, articulation, agreement. The Bible in all its parts conveys a revelation of God that is absolutely harmonious in every part, from beginning to end. If, however, our interpretations, or preconceived ideas and beliefs, are forced upon the Bible then the harmony is abruptly interrupted and the whole message comes to a screeching halt! Yet when the Bible is allowed to simply say what it says, and we accept it, everything flows together beautifully and there is no resistance at all. No agitating friction!

HARMONY IN THE GOSPELS

Over the years many have struggled and failed to find the harmony between the Gospels, and then the Gospels and the rest of the writings of the New Testament. One reason for this failure to find harmony is because people lack a biblical understanding of the kingdom and how good works are related. If the distinction between heaven and the kingdom is made, then the remaining writings of the New Testament flow perfectly with all four Gospels: the teaching of Jesus.

All four Gospels are written as records of the life of Jesus Christ; each Gospel has unique emphasis. The first three (Matthew, Mark, and Luke) historically have been identified as the Synoptic Gospels, and are distinct from the fourth, the Gospel of John.

Synoptic means to "present an account from the same point of view."[1] While differing slightly in emphasis (and audience), Matthew, Mark, and Luke each present a historical account of the life and ministry of Jesus. In so doing, they record Jesus offering a kingdom, being rejected, and the consequent postponing of the kingdom, which now becomes our future hope.

John, on the other hand, is not so concerned with historical chronology or end times; his emphasis is about eternal life *NOW.* John's Gospel is much more selective in recording the miraculous works and teachings from Jesus that conveyed the message of eternal life by faith alone. Here is his specific and uniquely stated purpose:

> Therefore many other signs Jesus also performed in the presence of the disciples, which are not written in this book; *but these have been written so that you may believe that Jesus is the Christ, the Son of God; and that believing you may have life in His name.*[2]

Matthew, Mark, and Luke all have a more historical approach and the concept of the kingdom is clearly evident as *the* central theme. A simple comparison of the number of times the word *kingdom* is used clearly illustrates this difference in emphasis:

Matthew: 55 times

Mark: 20 times

Luke: 46 times

John: **5 times**

While John uses the word kingdom only five times in two different contexts (chapters 3 and 18), he uses the word life thirty-six times (sixteen of which are together with the word eternal). It is clear from both his usage of terms and his stated purpose that John's emphasis is eternal salvation, not the kingdom as it is for Matthew, Mark, and Luke. It is a mistake to explain this difference as if Matthew, Mark, and Luke present the "earthly gospel" for Israel, while John presents the "heavenly gospel" for the church. While the distinctions are clearly evident, this conclusion is unnecessary and misleading. Harmony from the rest of the New Testament proves this point.

GOING DEEPER

From Acts through Revelation the term kingdom is used thirty-six times. Of those thirty-six usages, five are a reference to a kingdom man has established upon the earth or to a kingdom that Satan has established over the earth. The other thirty-one refer to God's kingdom. Those references include: The kingdom of God;[3] The kingdom of Christ and God;[4] The kingdom of His Beloved Son;[5] His kingdom;[6] His heavenly kingdom;[7] Kingdom of our Lord and Savior;[8] The kingdom of our God;[9] or simply kingdom[10] without any modifier. Of those thirty-one references to God's kingdom four (i.e., Romans 14:17; 1 Corinthians 4:20; Colossians 1:13; 2 Timothy 4:18) are typically misconstrued as something other than the earthly kingdom of Messiah. Those references, however, are not discussing a different kingdom, a spiritual kingdom, but even if they were, should the interpreter really be adamant in concluding that these four references demand a wholly different concept of kingdom from the other 27 references? Should four usages determine what the other

27 usages mean? That would mean that the interpreter must allow 12.9% of the usages to determine the concept of each reference to the kingdom instead of letting the 87.1% of the usages have any influence in determining meaning. And if 87.1% of the usages in Acts through Revelation carry the same meaning as all the usages in the Gospels, is it likely that the four usages, that might be understood differently, have the authority to overturn the others? I think not.

The writings of the New Testament take these two distinctions, from the Synoptic Gospels and the Gospel of John, and blend them into one agreeable harmony.

Let it say what it says…it is sweet to the ear.

HARMONY IN ETERNAL SALVATION

The first and most obvious note of harmony in the epistles is that which is found consistent with John's Gospel: *that salvation is by grace through faith alone.* In the Gospel of John, one clear and very well known example of this harmony is seen in the summary of Jesus' dialogue with a Pharisee named Nicodemus. In chapter 3 we read:

> God so loved the world that He gave His only begotten Son, that whoever believes in Him shall not perish, but have eternal life.[11]

God so *loved*…

That He *gave*…

That whoever *believes*…

Shall not perish, but have *everlasting life*…

That is a clear proclamation of salvation by grace through faith alone. In John's Gospel the only condition ever put upon the issue of eternal salvation is faith. These truths can be set right alongside Paul's statement that "God, being rich in mercy, because of His great love with which He loved us, even when we were dead in our transgressions, made us alive together with Christ (by grace you have been saved)...for by grace you have been saved through faith."[12]

Even though John uses the word *grace* only four times in one context, the idea is obvious throughout his Gospel: salvation is free.

Paul adds beautiful harmony to John when he indicates that it was His love which became visible through grace.[13] Understanding grace, as Charles Swindoll so aptly wrote, "requires our going back to an old Hebrew term that meant 'to bend, to stoop.' By and by, it came to include the idea of 'condescending favor.'"[14] Therefore, Swindoll continued, "grace is love that stoops."[15] Grace is God's demonstration of "His own love toward us, in that while we were yet sinners, Christ died for us."[16] The gift "costs the giver, not the recipient."[17]

The only condition to the recipient is that he believe!

No other condition is ever added to eternal salvation anywhere in the Bible.

And if any additional conditions are added to the gracious gift of God, then:

"You have fallen from grace,"[18] or

"Grace is no longer grace."[19]

If good works, repentance, righteous living, etc., are added to eternal salvation, then *HARMONY SCREECHES TO A HALT!*

Where the church has left this harmony is on the relationship of good works, declaring in sometimes subtle ways that good works are proof of, or required for, salvation. But as we will see here again, the harmony continues uninterrupted in all the Bible in dealing with good works.

The same message is found in every other book in the New Testament.

HARMONY OF HOLINESS

Jesus taught about the importance of living a righteous life and doing good works. The Synoptic Gospels do a thorough job of presenting this fact clearly, as does John's Gospel in any discussion on discipleship. However, Jesus never once said we needed to do good works to earn our eternal salvation; He never said we needed to do good works to legitimize our salvation; He never (not once) said we need to do good works to prove we are children of the Father.

> *Jesus never associated good works with eternal salvation.*

I hope you grasp the importance of this statement.

Jesus *never* associated good works with eternal salvation or assurance of eternal salvation.

What Jesus did teach was that good works done in faith are necessary for His committed followers; they prove who are His committed followers; and they are the means to earn rewards or a rulership role in the kingdom. In the Gospels, good works are always associated with discipleship and the kingdom. Yes, always!

So basically, if you do good works *in faith*, then you are a *committed follower* of Christ; others will be able to see that, and you will receive rewards for those works in the kingdom.

HARMONY IN PAUL

According to Paul, as recipients of salvation we are in God's eternal love and nothing can "separate us from the love of God, which is in Christ Jesus."[20] We can't pay Him back, prove our worthiness (for we were not worthy), or do any good work to affect the divine declaration: "by grace you have been saved."[21]

It is simply wrong to think that what we do has any bearing on our eternal salvation. As pastor and author Ed Underwood said,

> It's so absurd to receive grace and then try to pay Him back with works. What do you have to offer? Everything good about you was put into you by His grace.[22]

Yet as a redeemed child of God you are now His artistic expression: His "workmanship, created in Christ Jesus *for* good works."[23] While you don't *automatically* walk in them, you "*should* walk in them."[24] When we do walk in them by faith we become an expression of His love, grace, and power and we fulfill His calling and choosing. And if we do walk in those good works prepared for us, there is great reward.

The prize is not His love (because we can't earn that), but kingdom participation and reward.

THE KINGDOM IS THE PRIZE

Just as Jesus taught that entering the kingdom with full inheritance and great rewards to rule in the kingdom were privileges that must be earned,[25] so too do Paul and other New Testament writers. In fact, the idea of rewards and our inheritance in the coming kingdom was a primary motivation and means of accountability.

On more than one occasion Paul reminded churches about the coming accountability which all believers will face at the "judgment seat of Christ."[26] So let's stop right there and think about this: if our salvation is by grace and grace alone, and we can't work our way to salvation, then what's the point of the judgment seat? What's the point of Jesus looking at all of my deeds and telling me how I did with all He entrusted to me?

At this time, at judgment, "each one of us will give an account of himself to God."[27] The accounting will be to "test the quality of each man's work."[28] And the purpose of this judgment is to "receive a reward,"[29] "so that each one may be recompensed for his deeds in the body, according to what he has done, whether good or bad."[30]

The judgment of believers is for reward, not our eternal destiny. The accounting has nothing to do with eternal salvation, sin's penalty, redemption, or God's love. Jesus taught that the one who believes Him for the gift of eternal salvation does not come into judgment to decide where he will spend eternity.[31] And Paul heartily agreed when he wrote that nothing "will be able to separate us from the love of God, which is in Christ Jesus,"[32] the divine, unconditional love that provided the payment in Christ's death for our sins.

The bēma ("judgment seat" in Greek) is a judgment of a believer's works. If the works fail the test or prove of poor quality (e.g., a deed done for the wrong motive) and are "burned up, he will suffer loss."[33] What we lose is reward, not eternity.

Charles Stanley comments on this verse when he writes, "Keep in mind we are not talking about heaven and hell. That is a different issue altogether. Our works have nothing to do with *where* we spend eternity."[34]

We are accountable for our works.

PAUL'S EXAMPLE

Paul not only taught accountability to others, but he also *walked the walk*. In his first letter to the church at Corinth, Paul uses himself as an example of how important it is to live a consistent and disciplined life for fear of being "disqualified"[35] from rewards (in this case, a "crown" or "wreath"[36]) in the kingdom.

Paul said that we must all "run in such a way that you may

win."[37] He then went on to state, "Therefore *I* run in such a way, as not without aim; *I* box in such a way, as not beating the air; but *I* discipline *my* body and make it *my* slave, so that, after I have preached to others, *I* myself will not be disqualified."[38] Paul was clear that the possibility of disqualification still existed for him, an eternally saved individual.

Paul understood the importance of both living with purpose and the coming accountability.

If the kingdom is a reward that must be earned, it should make perfect sense that our inheritance is something we could be disqualified from. As God's sons we are "fellow heirs" and the kingdom is our inheritance, but that does not mean we will automatically get those riches.

DISQUALIFIED

In the end Satan will certainly lose the war, but along the way he steals minor victories when he can keep us from the kingdom or our rewards. Satan's greatest wish is to keep Christians from inheriting the kingdom. Satan's delight is to diminish the glory to God that is to come in a multitude of His trophies in the kingdom.

Those who fall prey to the deceitful lies and temptations of Satan fall into the trap of thinking we have nothing to live for, no hope, and nothing to be accountable for. The kinds of people who fall for this trick, described by Paul as those whose lives are characterized by sin, will therefore be disqualified and "will not inherit the kingdom."[39]

This statement poses no problem with the doctrine of salvation by grace through faith, or the eternal security of the believer, if we simply maintain the distinction between heaven/eternity with God and the kingdom. The issue of not inheriting is one of reward and the inheritance God wants to share with us in the coming kingdom.

GOING DEEPER

"Will not inherit the kingdom." This statement, "will not inherit [future tense] the kingdom," is found in 1 Corinthians 6:10 and Galatians 5:21; a similar statement, "no idolater has [present tense] an inheritance in the kingdom of Christ and God," is found in Ephesians 5:5. All three of these passages, in letters written by Paul to churches, are commonly called Vice List passages. The question many wrestle with is whether these passages speak of unbelievers or believers. The question is *not* whether the passages apply to believers, because Paul is writing to churches, so each passage serves as a warning to believers.

If the distinction is maintained between eternal salvation and the kingdom (as we have clearly shown exists in Scripture), then much of the perceived problem quickly vanishes. These passages are talking about inheritance in the coming kingdom (the prize), not eternal salvation (the gift).

Even if someone was to reason that the lists of people in the Corinthian and Ephesian passages refer to unbelievers, which is certainly by no means clear, the first question which must be asked is: Then what is the point of the warning? Answer: None! But this simply does not make sense. The point of the warning is that if the believers in either church follow the examples listed and live (i.e., are characterized by) sinful lives (which the church at Corinth certainly already was; seen clearly in 1 Corinthians 5:1–13), they will "not inherit [in the future] the kingdom" (1 Corinthians 6:10; Ephesians 5:5).

The applicability of this statement to believers is even clearer in the Galatians passage because the direct admonition is for them to "walk by the Spirit" so that "you [the Galatian believers] will not carry out the desire of the flesh" (Galatians 5:16). The one who does not walk by the Spirit is the one who will, by default, carry out the fleshly desires and produce "deeds of the flesh…[and] those who *practice* [i.e, are characterized by] such things will not [future tense] inherit the kingdom of God" (Galatians 5:19–21, emphasis mine). Not inheriting the kingdom is synonymous with losing reward or forfeiting inheritance in the coming kingdom.[40]

The warning in all three of these passages is severe and ought to be taken seriously by all believers, who by way of their son status have an inheritance in the coming kingdom. But that inheritance can be forfeited if the obligations are not met in righteous Spirit-led faithful living. Motivation?

The kingdom, our inheritance, can be forfeited.

Any system of rewards implies the need for accountability and inspection. My wife always reminds me that kids only do what you *inspect*, not what you *expect*.

Makes sense!

When the New Testament writings speak about loss, or losing

something, it is never about eternal salvation. It is about rewards, inheritance, and kingdom. Yet even in the face of loss of rewards or inheritance, every believer will be "saved, yet so as through fire."[41]

The reward of our inheritance comes in great variety.

VARIETY OF REWARD

Jesus taught that rewards come in a variety of manifestations: entering (or exclusion from) the kingdom,[42] celebration,[43] praise,[44] and rulership.[45] The same idea is expressed by many of the other writers of the New Testament.

CROWNS

One reward, which is discussed in a number of different contexts, is crowns that will be awarded to the believer for any number of reasons. A crown may be given because of the many lives that a person has affected by his ministry;[46] or because he has lived with an eternal perspective, watching eagerly for the Lord's return;[47] or because he has persevered in love through trials;[48] or because he has shepherded the flock of God selflessly in all humility;[49] or simply for exercising self-control and finishing the race.[50] The first a crown of exaltation; the second a crown of righteousness; the third a crown of life; the fourth a crown of glory; the fifth an imperishable crown!

I am not real big on adornments, but those sound pretty special.

Many people have downplayed the importance of such crowns

thinking that we, like the twenty-four elders,[51] will cast down our crowns at the feet of Jesus. Erwin Lutzer, author and pastor of Moody Church in Chicago, commented on this very thing:

> If we are given actual crowns in heaven, I'm sure that we shall gladly lay them at Christ's feet. But it is wrong to think that our rewards are crowns and nothing more. If we join the elders in casting our crowns before Him, I believe He shall give them back to us so we can join Him in ruling...[52]

Lutzer has certainly captured by his statement the truth of 2 Timothy 2:12, which affirms that as a believer perseveres or endures in a faithful walk of obedience, he will reign with Christ in the coming kingdom.

Crowns are what kings and queens wear. Crowns are important, just like every other reward Jesus will give to us, because they are our part in the inheritance among the sons of light/saints of light in the coming kingdom.[53] The crowns call believers to faithful service now so that they might join Christ later in His rule over His kingdom.

REALM OF RULE

While God wants all of His children to rule, He may deny some the right to rule with Christ if they deny Him.[54]

In the book of Revelation, John harmonizes perfectly, as seen in the promises of kingdom rewards given to "he who overcomes." While some of these rewards promised are indiscernible, or debatable, many others are not. Among them are such things as:

"I will give authority over the nations; and he shall rule them with a rod of iron." (2:26–27)

"I will confess his name before My Father." (3:5)

"I will grant him to sit down with Me on My throne, as I also overcame and sat down with My Father on His throne." (3:21)

Authority, confession (praise), ruling, and sitting on thrones are rewards to be realized in the coming kingdom of Messiah. To not overcome is to forfeit the reward.

This idea of reward in the kingdom or loss of reward receives much emphasis in the book of Hebrews.

HEBRAIC HARMONY

"And now you know...the rest of the story." This was Paul Harvey's closing tagline to his weekly broadcast, *The Rest of the Story*.

In the book of Hebrews, the rest of the story is *His rest*. The story is all about the long anticipated *rest*.

The concept of rest in the book of Hebrews is not a synonym for heaven or eternal salvation; nor is it about the experience of the Christian life today. The rest, spoken of in the book of Hebrews, is a synonym for the coming Messianic age. It is "His rest"[55] we enter, but it is also rest from our work.[56] Because of the Fall work is today "by the sweat of your face."[57] Or as Solomon said "all his days his task is painful and grievous; even at night his mind does not rest. This too is vanity."[58] *His rest* will be paradise regained.

Much ink has been spilled trying to reconcile difficult passages in the book of Hebrews, but the answer lies in the distinction of the *rest*.

The danger of concluding that *rest* refers to heaven should be obvious; if *rest* is synonymous with heaven then we must persevere, be diligent, do good works so that we can be good enough to enter heaven. This is totally unnecessary and dangerous. And Satan would like nothing more than to cause Christians to be insecure about their eternal destiny so that they busy themselves performing for God so that they can go to heaven (when in reality that issue is already dealt with and guaranteed).

It is a trick Satan plays...don't buy into it!

This would be like my biological son doing his chores so that he could be my son. The chores have nothing to do with my relation to him or my commitment to him; and in the same fashion, what we do for God has no bearing on the security of our relationship to Him or His commitment to us.

Satan knows he can't alter our eternal destiny, so his efforts focus more on keeping us from the prize: the *rest* (our reward).

I hope and pray that we are all way too smart to buy into that lie of Satan.

SO WHAT IS THE REST?

The original concept of "rest" spoken of in Hebrews ties analogously to the historical warning given to the nation of Israel when they came out of Egypt. Because the nation was disobedient, God did not permit them to enter the Promised Land and have rest.[59] In the Old Testament the "rest" that is repeatedly spoken of is both geographical and situational. The geographical location of the *rest* was the Promised Land.[60] But the situational rest is "from all your enemies...so that you live in security."[61]

As Jody Dillow comments, "Rest is the inheritance, but it is also a condition or state of finished work and victory over enemies."[62]

The historical *rest* was possession of the land and deliverance from enemies, but that *rest* concept took on a prophetic nuance when the prophets spoke of a future *rest*, the Messianic kingdom. Daniel describes a future "time of distress,"[63] after which he states, "You will enter into rest and rise again to your allotted portion at the end of the age."[64] And the prophet Ezekiel as well makes the connection of future rest to the coming Messianic kingdom.[65]

A person of Jewish descent would have had a thorough working knowledge of the idea of prophetic *rest* as spoken of in the Old Testament. It therefore makes perfect sense in a letter written to Hebrew Christians that the rest being spoken of is a reference to the coming Messianic age: the kingdom.

The Hebrew Christians being addressed in this letter are admonished to "be diligent to enter that rest, so that no one will fall [short], through following the same example of disobedience."[66]

Rest is a reward earned by faithful, diligent obedience!

Disobedience, on the other hand, is the cause for failing to enter God's rest and realize the full reward. The emphasis in the whole book of Hebrews is on perseverance and the diligence that can be rewarded with the fulfillment of the promises God has given.[67]

This is confirmed in chapter 11, the chapter of faithful obedience, where those listed did not receive the reward and inheritance of what was promised because God had "provided something better for us."[68] What is better for us is the coming kingdom, because it will be significantly better than anything or any time in the past.

That this *rest* is synonymous with the coming kingdom is clear in the book where we find the instruction that "through faith and patience" the promises given to Abraham will be inherited.[69] The Abrahamic promises are repeatedly throughout the whole Bible tied to the Messianic hope in the kingdom. Those promises will certainly be realized in the kingdom when "Christ...will appear a second time for salvation without reference to sin, to those who eagerly await Him."[70] This salvation spoken of here is future, and refers to the final deliverance of those who enter the rest.

The author of Hebrews, like Paul, makes it clear that the rest can be lost or that a believer may come short of even entering into that rest.[71] The only way to realize our share with Christ is to "hold fast the beginning of our assurance firm until the end."[72]

Perseverance is essential to realizing our share in the promised rest. Perseverance is not essential to remain in God's love. God will always persevere in His love toward us, because He is faithful.

IN THE END

The conclusion to the whole warning of Hebrews is seen in the final warning in chapter 12, where the author states that if we "refuse Him who is speaking...who warns from heaven," we shall not escape.[73] The question naturally arises to any reader: escape from what? Hell? Surely that is not the issue.

The answer lies in the text.

The writer of the book says that the reason for not refusing or turning away from God is because "we receive a kingdom which cannot be shaken."[74] For this reason we are to "show gratitude, by which we may offer to God an acceptable service with reverence and awe; for our God is a consuming fire."[75] The context indicates that the fire is a synonym for His loving discipline and chastisement.

The point of the whole book, warning passages and all, is that a kingdom is coming which will be a rest for the people of God and that all who remain faithful will inherit it. Thus, "we enter into rest only when we persevere in faith to the end of life. When we do this, we will obtain a share in the inheritance...and will rule with Christ."[76]

God would never hold eternal salvation over our heads as if we could lose it. Since God's rest can be lost, it cannot be a synonym for eternal salvation. The only thing that can be lost is the inheritance in the kingdom because it is something that is earned through diligent faithful obedience.

God has a wonderful plan for our lives. That plan is to grant you, through your diligent walk of faith, the coming kingdom which was prepared before the foundation of the world.

The kingdom? It was always God's plan for the earth! Just as Jesus taught.

> *God would never hold eternal salvation over our heads.*

SINGING THE SWEET TUNE

Not only are the ideas of the kingdom and rest for all who persevere harmonious with the Scriptures; they are also in harmony with who we know our heavenly Father to be: one who rewards His beloved from His great abundance and wealth.

Peter reminds us that we are born again to a hope that is alive because of Jesus' resurrection.[77] This hope, a future certainty, guarantees the availability of the promises of our future inheritance reserved in heaven for us.[78] Even though some might mock the idea of the certainty of His coming and consequently live immorally, we need to be holy in conduct, looking for and hastening the day, and diligent to be found by Him in peace, spotless and blameless.[79]

Or, as Peter states in his second epistle, you must put forth every bit of effort, and "in your faith supply moral excellence, and in your moral excellence, knowledge, and in your knowledge, self-control, and in your self-control, perseverance, and in your perseverance, godliness, and in your godliness, brotherly kindness, and in your brotherly kindness, love."[80] If we are diligent in developing these virtues, we fulfill our "calling and choosing," making them sure.[81] If we pursue these virtues diligently, when we enter His kingdom, He will lavish us with rewards.[82]

Hopefully you see, and hear, the sweet harmony that exists in the New Testament on eternal salvation by grace through faith alone; and that good works, faithfulness, and perseverance are for rewards in the kingdom. While what we have covered here may cause some disharmony with previous perspectives or interpretations, it is the most harmonious perspective with the Scriptures. The harmony ought to make you feel like I do, and so many others I know: free and yet extremely motivated.

The truth shall make you free...yes, free indeed.

That is a tune that is sweet to the ear.

NOTES

1 *Webster's II New College Dictionary*, 1ˢᵗ ed., s.v. "synoptic."
2 John 20:30–31.
3 Acts 1:3; 8:12; 14:22; 19:8; 28:23, 31; Romans 14:17; 1 Corinthians 6:9, 10; 15:24, 50; Galatians 5:21; Colossians 4:11; 2 Thessalonians 1:5
4 Ephesians 5:5
5 Colossians 1:13
6 2 Timothy 4:1; Hebrews 1:8
7 2 Timothy 4:18
8 2 Peter 1:11
9 Revelation 12:10
10 Acts 1:6; 20:25; 1 Thessalonians 2:12; Hebrews 12:28; James 2:5
11 John 3:16.
12 Ephesians 2:4–5, 8.
13 See Ephesians 2:4–5.
14 Charles R. Swindoll, "Understanding Grace," *Insight For Living*, Nov. 1, 2008.
15 Ibid.
16 Romans 5:8.
17 Charles C. Bing, *Simply by Grace*, 35
18 Galatians 5:4.
19 Romans 11:6.
20 Romans 8:39; see also 8:35.
21 Ephesians 2:5, 8.
22 Ed Underwood, "Lopsided Teaching About Grace?" *Ed Underwood: Radical Hope, Radical Christianity* (blog), February 13, 2010, http://edunderwood.com/2010/02/13/lopsided-teaching-about-grace/.
23 Ephesians 2:10, emphasis mine.
24 Ibid, NKJV, emphasis mine.
25 See Matthew 5:20; 18:3; 19:23–30.
26 2 Corinthians 5:10; see also Romans 14:10.
27 Romans 14:12.
28 1 Corinthians 3:13b.
29 1 Corinthians 3:14.
30 2 Corinthians 5:10.
31 See John 5:24.
32 Romans 8:39.
33 1 Corinthians 3:15.
34 Charles Stanley, *Eternal Security: Can You Be Sure?* (Nashville: Thomas Nelson Publishers, 2002), 119.
35 1 Corinthians 9:27.
36 1 Corinthians 9:25.
37 1 Corinthians 9:24.
38 1 Corinthians 9:26–27, emphasis mine.
39 See 1 Corinthians 6:9–10; Galatians 5:21; Ephesians 5:5.
40 See Matthew 19:16–30
41 1 Corinthians 3:15.

42 See Matthew 5:20; 8:12; 18:3; 25:30; Luke 13:28.
43 See Matthew 8:11; Luke 13:29; 22:30.
44 See Matthew 10:32; 25:21, 23; Luke 19:17.
45 See Matthew 19:28; 25:21, 23; Luke 19:17, 19; 22:30.
46 See 1 Thessalonians 2:19.
47 See 2 Timothy 4:8.
48 See James 1:12; Revelation 2:10.
49 See 1 Peter 5:2–3.
50 1 Corinthians 9:25.
51 See Revelation 4:10.
52 Erwin Lutzer, *Your Eternal Reward: Triumph and Tears at the Judgment Seat of Christ* (Chicago: Moody Publishers, 1998), 152.
53 See John 12:36; Colossians 1:12.
54 See 2 Timothy 2:12.
55 Hebrews 4:1
56 Hebrews 4:10
57 Genesis 3:19
58 Ecclesiastes 2:23
59 See Hebrews 3:7–19 (esp. vv. 18–19).
60 Deuteronomy 12:8–9; Psalm 95:11; 132:13–14.
61 Deuteronomy 12:10; see also Joshua 21:44.
62 Dillow, *Reign of the Servant Kings*, 98.
63 Daniel 12:1.
64 Daniel 12:13.
65 See Ezekiel 34:15, 20–25.
66 Hebrews 4:11.
67 See Hebrews 4:1; 6:12; 10:35–36.
68 Hebrews 11:40.
69 Hebrews 6:12–13.
70 Hebrews 9:28.
71 See Hebrews 4:1.
72 See Hebrews 3:14.
73 Hebrews 12:25.
74 Hebrews 12:28.
75 Hebrews 12:28–29.
76 Dillow, *Reign of the Servant Kings*, 109.
77 See 1 Peter 1:3.
78 See 1 Peter 1:4.
79 See 2 Peter 3:2–4, 10–14.
80 2 Peter 1:5–7.
81 2 Peter 1:10.
82 See 2 Peter 1:5–7, 11.

FIFTEEN

HIS GLORY ACCOMPLISHED

Man's soul search indicates that something he previously possessed is missing.

Myles Munroe

Saturday, December 10, 2010 was one of those days I'd soon like to forget.

It was a long planned and eagerly anticipated day of golf. The tournament had been on my calendar for months. The day did not, however, go at all like I planned or hoped. It started off when I awoke to the sound of pouring rain. Undeterred, I gathered my rain gear and set off early to meet my golf partner and load his golf cart onto my trailer.

After twenty minutes in the rain loading and securing the cart I received word that the tournament was cancelled. Soaked, disappointed and a bit disgruntled, I headed home to help with Christmas decorations when I got a phone call. It was one of the elders from the church, "Bill passed away last night." Bill was one of the most hard-working, servant-hearted people I have ever had the pleasure to know.

I went to meet the family where many fond stories were shared, a service planned, and tears shed. After the meeting I began making calls to put the music together for the service. When I spoke with the fuller-than-life spunky gal that was the requested singer... something was not right. I inquired. She burst into tears and said, "We found out last night that Tim's [her husband] prostate is full of cancer." More tears were shed and prayers prayed.

Now I was completely numb.

A day planned and full of anticipation and excitement was interrupted by the effects of a fallen world and the dominion of darkness. Ugh!

I am sure you have had a day similar to the one I just described. Maybe you have had many: a whole string of these days you would soon like to forget.

Days like these serve as a sobering reminder of what we are missing today and what we are looking forward to in the future when the risen Lord of Glory, the King of kings, will come back to right every wrong, lift the curse, and once and for all put the devil and his kingdom in its place.

Take courage. The day is coming.

That future day will relieve all our disappointment, frustration, sadness, and longing. The Bible calls that day the "day of Christ,"[1] the "day of the Lord,"[2] and the day of the "Son of Man."[3] His day will come suddenly; and it will be as the sudden flashes of lighting in the sky.[4]

On my disappointing day, of which I am sure there are more to come, I was reminded of the words of Paul to the church at Rome: "I consider that the sufferings of this present time are not worthy to be compared with the glory that is to be revealed to us."[5]

Glory...*ah, yes*! That is what it is all about. And it will be glorious!

> *The risen Lord of Glory, the King of kings, will come back to right every wrong.*

And that day of glory is as certain as Christ is in us, "the hope of glory." This is our biblical hope: certain future expectation.

This is the hope of all creation.[6]

It is the hope we eagerly await.[7]

It is the hope of our calling.[8]

It is this hope that causes us to grieve differently than those who have none.[9]

It is this hope that must sober us and which we fix "completely on the grace to be brought to you at the revelation of Jesus Christ."[10]

And here is how it's going to unfold.

A TIME YET TO COME

Jesus promised that He would not leave us as orphans,[11] but would personally return[12] to take us to be with Him where He is.[13] He will come for the church in the same fashion that He ascended[14] and the church will be "caught up" with Him in the air.[15] This is the first step for the church in realizing our hope. It is a time when "God will bring with Him those who have fallen asleep in Jesus," and they will "rise first."[16] And then "we who are alive and remain will be caught up together with them [the dead in Christ that rose first] in the clouds to meet the Lord in the air."[17]

This great snatch of all believers in the church to meet Jesus in the air is called the Rapture (from the Latin *rapturo;* a translation of the Greek *harpozo).*

After the Rapture of the church, a period of seven years of great distress and outpouring of the wrath of God on the earth will come.[18] This period of distress is called the "tribulation," and the "great tribulation."[19] This period will be the final week, a period of seven years, of Daniel's seventy-week (seventy periods of seven years) prophecy.[20]

The purpose of this period is to punish the evil Gentile nations who have long-oppressed Israel; and purge out a righteous remnant of that holy chosen nation.[21] This period of great distress will also be a period of great salvation of both Jew and Gentile.[22] Those saved during this time will be the ones who "come out of the great tribulation"[23] and will populate (and repopulate) the earth in the millennial kingdom.

At the end of that seven-year period, Christ will come back to this earth and His feet will touch down on the Mount of Olives[24] and He will begin His reign and be King over all the earth.[25] It is at that time when He will be "King of kings, and Lord of lords."[26] This return to earth will be a physical, visible return as it is described in the book of Revelation.

In Revelation we are given a detailed and elaborate account of the Tribulation in chapters 6 through 18, and then comes Messiah in triumph, because His return comes "after these things."[27] His coming will be preceded by a heavenly worship service described as a "great multitude in heaven, saying, 'Hallelujah! Salvation and glory and power belong to our God; because His judgments are true and righteous; for He has judged the great harlot who was corrupting the earth with her immorality, and He has avenged the blood of His bond-servants on her."[28]

It will be a day of great celebration, a worship service like no other.

Messiah's first coming was a royal presentation of the king; His second coming will be triumphant and unmistakably cataclysmic.

THE RETURN OF THE KING

When the king comes in His kingdom, and He is certain to come for the day is fixed,[29] it will be a coming that Daniel describes as a rock coming down from heaven smashing all the kingdoms of the earth (who are under the rule of the kingdom of darkness).[30] That stone that smashes the kingdoms of the earth becomes "a great mountain and [fills] the whole earth."[31] His sovereign dominion will be absolute.

This second coming of Messiah in triumph will bring an end to the times of the Gentiles[32] and their "dominion [will be] taken away."[33]

The tribulation is now complete; the earth is ready for the King. John hears another heavenly chorus sing, "Hallelujah! For the Lord our God, the Almighty reigns."[34]

And then comes this statement (*worth repeating in full*):

> And I saw heaven opened, and behold, a white horse, and He who sat on it is called Faithful and True, and in righteousness He judges and wages war. His eyes are a flame of fire, and on His head are many diadems; and He has a name written on Him which no one knows except Himself. He is clothed with a robe dipped in blood, and His name is called The Word of God.... From His mouth comes a sharp sword, so that with it He may strike down the nations, and He will rule them with a rod of iron; and He treads the wine press of the fierce wrath of God, the Almighty. And on His robe and on His thigh He has a name written, "KING OF KINGS, AND LORD OF LORDS."[35]

There is no greater description of the Son of Man!

This parallels Daniel's vision (*again, worth repeating in full*):

> I kept looking in the night visions, and behold, with the clouds of heaven one like a Son of Man was coming, and He came up to the Ancient of Days and

was presented before Him. And to Him was given dominion, glory and a kingdom, that all the peoples, nations, and men of every language might serve Him. His dominion is an everlasting dominion which will not pass away; and His kingdom is one which will not be destroyed.[36]

Here is our coming King in triumph!

Isaac Watts wrote the hymn "Joy to the World" as a paraphrase of Psalm 98, and he published it in his *Psalms of David Imitated* (1719) under the heading "The Messiah's Coming and Kingdom." Traditionally we sing this great hymn in celebration of Christ's first coming, yet Watts wrote the words glorifying Christ's triumphant return at the end of the age. "Joy to the world, the Lord has come!"

At this time of His triumphant return the beast, and the false prophet, will be seized and "thrown alive into the lake of fire."[37] This will bring an end to the deceptive influence they have had since the Fall. And the devil himself, Satan, will be bound and thrown into the abyss, where he will remain for the duration of the thousand-year portion of Messiah's reign on this earth.[38] The earth will be completely void of the devious snake, all his minions, and all his lies.

What a cause for rejoicing!

This triumph will be the contrast against which the Glory of God is displayed to its fullest degree because God will be present and the whole world will see and know. God is going to complete what He started before the foundation of the world. This period of

Messiah's rule will be the consummation of His glorious plan for this earth.

It will be the absolute and total defeat of the kingdom of darkness cast against the glory of the absolute victorious dominion of the kingdom of Christ. This is the storyline the Bible follows to its appropriate end, for "the Bible is the story of God's divinely determined plan to crush the rebellion and reclaim the kingdom in its entirety."[39]

This time will be the consummation, completion, and fulfillment of His glory on earth.

Nothing in history resembles such majesty and glory.

Even the earth itself longs for this day.[40]

We have been created with a longing for this glory. We "groan within ourselves" waiting this day of glory.[41] Nothing will satisfy our soul thirst until Jesus is on His throne.

In Revelation 19, after the glorious description of the one sitting on the white horse whose name is "Faithful and True,"[42] we read that "armies which are in heaven, clothed in fine linen, white and clean, were following Him on white horses."[43]

Who are those in the army? Hopefully you and me!

I am not much for war, but this one will be a little different (it may last less than a day!). Give me one of those white horses and clothe me in fine linen!

I am ready to ride!

In the next chapter Messiah's reign is set up and those who overcome and remain faithful are established in their positions of priestly rulership to reign with Christ throughout the age.[44]

This is the time when the saints will take possession of the kingdom of Messiah.[45] This is the fullness of salvation we await, but as Paul indicates every day we live that "salvation is nearer to us than when we believed."[46]

This is the hope of rest that we all strive to attain.[47]

Honestly now, that sounds pretty good, doesn't it?

When Jesus Christ returns for the second time it is upon this advent that the kingdom will be set up and His reign of unprecedented joy, peace, and righteousness will begin.

While Jesus is presently sitting at the right hand of the Father's throne, He will one day come back to earth to sit on His "glorious throne."[48]

While Jesus is presently serving as head over all things to the church,[49] all things will be subjected to Him in the Messianic age to come.[50]

> *He will sit on His "glorious throne."*

While Jesus is presently serving as our High Priest, when He comes He will serve as the Priest-King.

The day is drawing near. That is worth living diligently for.

Paul tells us that because the day is drawing near we must:

> Lay aside the deeds of darkness and put on the armor of light. Let us behave properly as in the day, not in carousing and drunkenness, not in sexual promiscuity and sensuality, not in strife and jealousy. But put on the Lord Jesus Christ, and make no provision for the flesh in regard to its lusts.[51]

DON'T LOSE HEART

You and I are going to have many days on this earth we would soon like to forget. We may struggle to be patient as we endure the effects of this fallen world. We may grieve much over the many moments of pain, suffering and loss, but we do not "grieve as do the rest who have no hope."[52] Don't lose heart. Don't lose focus. Don't lose hope. The day will come...God has a plan and while to the Lord "one day is like a thousand years, and a thousand years like one day...the Lord is not slow about His promise...the day of the Lord will come like a thief."[53]

What sort of people ought we to be?

We ought to be people "looking for and hastening the coming of the day of God."[54]

We ought to be people who are "diligent to be found by Him in peace, spotless and blameless, and regard the patience of our Lord as salvation."[55]

He is coming.

His glory will be fully accomplished!

NOTES

1 Philippians 2:16.
2 1 Thessalonians 5:2; 2 Peter 3:10.
3 Daniel 7:13; Matthew 24:30, 39, 42, 44.
4 See Matthew 24:27; Luke 24:27.
5 Romans 8:18.
6 See Romans 8:19–23.
7 See Romans 8:25.
8 See Ephesians 1:18; 4:4.
9 See 1 Thessalonians 4:13; Ephesians 2:2.
10 1 Peter 1:13.
11 See John 14:3.
12 See John 14:3; 18b.
13 See John 14:3b.
14 See Acts 1:11.
15 See 1 Thessalonians 4:17.
16 1 Thessalonians 4:14, 16.
17 1 Thessalonians 4:17.
18 See Daniel 12:1; Joel 2:2; Habakkuk 3:16; Zephaniah 1:15; Luke 21:23.
19 See Matthew 24:9, 21.
20 See Daniel 9:27.
21 See Daniel 12:1; Matthew 24:31.
22 See Revelation 7:9.
23 Revelation 7:14.
24 See Zechariah 14:4.
25 See Zechariah 14:9.
26 1 Timothy 6:15; Revelation 19:16.
27 Revelation 19:1.
28 Revelation 19:1–2.
29 See Habakkuk 2:3.
30 See 2:44–45.
31 Daniel 2:35.
32 See Luke 21:24; Romans 11:25.
33 Daniel 7:12.
34 Revelation 19:6.
35 Revelation 19:11–13, 15–16.
36 Daniel 7:13–14.
37 Revelation 19:20.
38 See Revelation 20:1–3.
39 Weber, *Holman New Testament Commentary: Matthew,* 7.
40 See Romans 8:18–22.
41 Romans 8:23.
42 Revelation 19:11.

43 Revelation 19:14.
44 See Revelation 20:4, 6.
45 See Daniel 7:22.
46 Romans 13:11.
47 See Daniel 12:13; Hebrews 4:1.
48 Matthew 25:31.
49 Ephesians 1:22.
50 Ephesians 1:21; Hebrews 1:8–13; 2:8; Revelation 3:21.
51 Romans 13:12–14.
52 1 Thessalonians 4:13.
53 2 Peter 3:8–10.
54 2 Peter 3:12; see all 3:14.
55 2 Peter 3:14–15.

SIXTEEN

WHAT TO DO NOW?

The mass of men lead lives of quiet desperation.

Henry David Thoreau

From the opening pages of Genesis to the closing chapter of Revelation, the main theme of the Bible is the kingdom of God. Through sixty-six books written by forty-plus authors over a period of sixteen hundred years, there is one great and marvelous unifying theme. The evidence is overwhelming that from eternity past God has been in the process of establishing His kingdom on earth as it is in heaven. And His kingdom will come!

In light of the evidence the only appropriate question is: *What do we do now?* Or: *Where do we go from here?*

To begin let us be reminded of what we should not do, or where we should *not* go.

We should not simply become more religious. We should not decide or determine to simply pull ourselves up by our own bootstraps and get busy for God. There is plenty to do, but we must remember that the Bible clearly teaches that we can't do it on our own. As Paul stated, "I know that nothing good dwells in me, that is, in my flesh; for the wishing [to do] is present in me, but the doing of the good is not."[1] We simply do not have the capacity in our own resources to do what needs to be done.

So being a religious zealot is not the answer.

The answer is: we must "walk by faith, not by sight."[2] To do that we desperately need to "draw near to God"[3] and "walk in newness of life."[4]

The new life is the very life of Jesus Christ which indwells us through the presence and power of the Holy Spirit. The only way to tap His resource in us is to walk by faith. Understanding his own incapability and Christ's capability is what caused Paul to say, "I have been crucified with Christ; and it is no longer I who live, but Christ lives in me; and the life which I now live in the flesh I live by faith in the Son of God, who loved me and gave Himself up for me."[5]

Faith is essential in our walk because "without faith it is impossible to please Him."[6] Faith is the means that we "walk in the Light as He Himself is in the Light...[that] we have fellowship with one another."[7] It is a relationship.

Jesus gave us a beautiful agricultural picture of this very thing when He said, "Abide in Me [the Vine], and I in you. As the branch cannot bear fruit of itself unless it abides in the vine, so neither can you unless you abide in Me."[8] Abiding is simply another picture of faith. And Jesus went on to say, "Apart from Me you can do nothing."[9] While we can be busy, we cannot be worthy apart from faith because "whatever is not from faith is sin."[10] Faith is the means through which we draw Christ's life.

We don't need more gimmicks. We don't need a new method, or the latest Christian fad. What we need is Jesus.

But we must also remember that he "who comes [by faith] to God must believe that He is and that He is a rewarder of those who seek Him."[11] God wants to reward those who seek Him. So my encouragement to you is to let the word of the kingdom sink deep into the soil of your heart and walk with Jesus, that you might be moved and motivated and bear fruit.

That's right. Let all that you have learned just sink in and trust God and He will use the knowledge you have gained to motivate you. Then you will "seek first His kingdom and His righteousness."[12]

HAVING GONE...MAKE DISCIPLES

In times past, the first thing a nurse would do to a newborn baby is induce a cry by holding it upside down and slapping its backside or pinching its foot. The cry is a sign of life.

The absence of that newborn cry is cause for concern and a source of fretful moments for new parents. That first cry is evidence that the amniotic fluid has exited the lungs and the baby is breathing normally on its own. From that point on, however, the cry of a baby indicates that the baby either needs something or wants something. It is his only way of communicating and is essential to life.

But not forever!

Hopefully, babies grow to be children, and then teens, and finally mature adults. At some time in that process, hopefully sooner than later, this kind of crying stops. We grow up and learn new ways to communicate and we learn that we don't always get everything we want.

When we come into this world we are naturally and inherently oriented to self. Self is all we know. Selfishness is natural. It is what we inherit from our father and mother, who inherited it from theirs and so on all the way back to Adam and Eve.[13] It is a result of the Fall.

As we progress from infancy to childhood, this inclination does not change automatically. Children still think they deserve everything, or that everything is owed to them. When they don't get what they want, they wail...*whah*!

There's a song by the group Down Here called "The Problem," and it is humorous but true. The song starts by theorizing about how the world is filled with misery. The group, being from Canada, suggests in jest that they will "write to [their] prime minister and you write your president" in an effort to help correct the problem. Then the chorus begins, "Everybody's wondering how the world could get this way, if God is good, then how could it be filled with so much pain? It's not the age-old mystery we've made it out to be, yeah there's a problem with the world, the problem with the world is ME." *Aha*. Truth.

The song goes on to explain when this problem ("ME") started: "No one taught me how to put myself first, it came so very naturally, I'M NOT A PRODIGY." Funny, but so true! None of us are prodigies at selfishness. We are all experts at selfishness and it does come naturally.

This is why Proverbs instructs parents to "Train up a child in the way he should go."[14] If children are not trained in the way they should go, they will naturally go their own way (the way they want to go), which is selfish; they will think they deserve everything, or that everything is owed to them. This child training is to "give wisdom, but a child who gets his own way brings shame to his mother."[15]

Lack of training is why we see so many grown adults throwing tantrums when they don't get their way!

What a shame.

When we come to Jesus we are born again and are "infants in Christ."[16] As infants we can only handle milk, but we are not supposed to stay in that state; we are to grow up and become mature.[17] We need to move past milk to meat. We too need to grow into mature adult children of God. We need to become disciples of Jesus: fully committed followers of Christ.

Growing up is an essential of discipleship. We must grow up to be productive.

Becoming a child of the heavenly Father is free; it has no cost to us (although it cost Him dearly). Being a disciple of Jesus Christ our Lord, however, has great costs and requires many sacrifices, but also comes with promise of great reward.

The two—becoming a child of God (receiving the gift of salvation through faith alone) and being a disciple (who earns the prize of the kingdom reward through works done in faith)—are fundamentally different and yet wonderfully connected. God gives us new life freely as a gift, but to find the full flavor of that life in our experience today and in the future, we must be willing to count the cost and surrender all.

Growth is at the heart of discipleship. In fact, the term translated as "disciple" is from the Greek word *mathetes*, which is where we get the word *mathematics*. The word *mathetes* signifies one who is a learner or a follower of a teacher, master, or lord.

So discipleship is about learning and following the Lord Jesus.

That is why discipleship, not getting people to heaven, is the real emphasis. Jesus did say, "Go therefore and *make disciples* of all the nations."[18] Getting the good news of Jesus' death and resurrection to lost souls is assumed here ("go" is an aorist participle and should be translated as "having gone"), so we should not overlook the task. We must be His "witnesses...even to the remotest part of the earth."[19] To be His witnesses assumes the inclusion of His death, burial, and resurrection, but it must also include the fact that He will return at the time which the Father has "fixed by His own authority."[20] One need only believe Christ for the offer of eternal salvation provided freely on the basis of His death and resurrection in order to be eternally saved; but what added motivation, to witness also of His imminent return to reign! Who wouldn't want to be on that team?

Sadly, in our day witnessing for Christ has become a forgotten piece of our responsibility and privilege. In fact, it has even become taboo.

We have been entrusted with the beautiful "word of reconciliation"[21]. We ought to proclaim it to everyone. But making converts is not the end goal and won't satisfy. Jesus wants converts (spiritual infants) made into committed disciples.

Jesus said that disciples are *made* by "baptizing...[and] teaching them to observe all that I commanded."[22] Becoming a disciple of Jesus Christ is on-the-job training for which there is great reward in the coming kingdom. Jesus made the kingdom an integral part of discipleship.

DISCIPLESHIP AND THE KINGDOM

When Jesus called Simon, who is called Peter, and Andrew his brother, His plan was to make them "fishers of men."[23] The first task of His disciples was to assist in offering the kingdom and *reeling* the nation of Israel into the kingdom.[24] This call to be fishermen is explained in a prophecy given six hundred years prior by the prophet Jeremiah about the future hope of Israel. Jeremiah records the Lord's promises to Israel as follows:

> "Behold, days are coming," declares the LORD, "when...I will restore them to their own land which I gave to their fathers. Behold, I am going to send for many fishermen," declares the LORD, "and they will fish for them."[25]

The historical context of this promise was the prophecy of God's future restoration of the nation of Israel back to the Promised Land in the Messianic age.

And, Jesus did not stop there either.

After looking on the multitudes and feeling compassion for them, for they were sheep without a shepherd, He said to the disciples, "The harvest is plentiful, but the workers are few. Therefore beseech the Lord of the harvest to send out workers into His harvest."[26] Again our roots in the Old Testament help us understand that this imagery of harvest was a precipitating event before the promised kingdom.[27] This is the time the fortunes of Israel would be restored.[28] Since the harvest was ready, Jesus instructed the disciples,

> "Do not go in the way of Gentiles, and do not enter any city of the Samaritans; but rather go to the lost sheep of the house of Israel. And as you go, preach, saying, 'The kingdom of heaven is at hand.' Heal the sick, raise the dead, cleanse the lepers, cast out demons."[29]

An essential part of the discipleship process was to preach the kingdom and reel people back to God so that they could participate in the Messianic age.

Things have not changed. We don't need new church growth methods or new gimmicks, we need to share the good news of Jesus' death and resurrection and the good news of the kingdom and the coming King. We need to proclaim both gospels.

That's right. We need to preach two gospels: the gospel of eternal salvation by faith alone and the gospel of the kingdom. In short, "be [His] witnesses...even to the remotest part of the earth."[30]

The harvest is *ripe*...so let's keep *reeling* people into the kingdom!

DISCIPLESHIP JESUS' WAY

Jesus journeyed with the Twelve and continually taught them important issues related to being a disciple. This is seen in His instruction, which immediately followed His commission to preach the gospel of the kingdom.

What did He teach them?

He taught them that the way of discipleship would be one of persecution similar to the kind of persecution He would face.[31] He taught them that the only way to "[endure] to the end"[32] was to live in reverence and surrender to Him.[33] What does that mean? What does that look like?

Jesus explained that a disciple is one who "confesses Me before men"[34] despite what persecution may come as a result. Confessing Jesus is the public acknowledgement of His royal identity. The disciple who does such will receive the reward of commendation from Jesus to the Father, for Jesus said, "I will confess him before the Father." This commendation is the equivalent of hearing, "Well done, My good and faithful servant."[35] This is the same idea that is promised to the one who overcomes in Revelation.[36]

Adversely, failure to publicly announce Jesus as the king would lead to loss. Jesus explained this when He said, "Whoever denies Me before men, I will also deny him before My Father."[37] Paul has the same idea in mind when he writes to Timothy, "If we endure we will also reign with Him; if we deny Him, He also will deny us."[38] His denial of us means losing the reward of reigning with Him in His kingdom.

Relationship is a gift. Ruling is a reward!

Jesus also told them that being His disciple might bring division of family and other close relationships. He said, "He who loves father or mother more than Me is not worthy of Me; and he who loves son or daughter more than Me is not worthy of Me. And he who does not take up his own cross and follow after Me is not worthy of Me. He who has found his life will lose it, and he who has lost his life for My sake will find it."[39] Or as Luke records, "If anyone comes to Me, and does not hate his own father and mother and wife and children and brothers and sisters, yes, even his own life, he cannot be My disciple."[40]

Now before you rush to judgment, stop and deliberate for just a moment.

First, does Jesus mean hate in the way we understand hate today?

And second, could this really somehow be about becoming a Christian?

> *Relationship is a gift.*
>
> *Ruling is a reward.*

The answer to both questions is: No!

Hating can be understood as "love less" or "to be indifferent in comparison."

And losing your life, hating father or mother, taking up your cross, or hating your own life are *not* conditions for eternal salvation, but *are* conditions of discipleship.

Being a disciple of Jesus Christ requires serious commitment and a willingness to surrender all. Since there are obvious costs and conditions that are more than and differ from faith, this cannot be about how to become a Christian. As Dr. Charles Bing stated so clearly, "The stringent conditions Christ attached to this sense of discipleship should not be made conditions of salvation, but should move us who are Christians further into God's will."[41]

This commitment that Jesus is calling His disciples to, which we should follow as well, is a commitment that will be rewarded in the kingdom. This is the wage; that which is earned.

This connection is clearly seen in a parallel passage when Jesus said to His disciples, "If anyone wishes to come after Me, he must deny himself, and take up his cross and follow Me. For whoever wishes to save his life will lose it; but whoever loses his life for My sake will find it...*for the Son of Man is going to come in the glory of His Father with His angel, and will then repay every man according to his deeds*."[42] The time when Jesus is going to come in glory and with His angels is His second coming at the end of the age, the time of harvest, to set up His kingdom.[43] That is the time when disciples will be rewarded according to their deeds (done in faith).

Being a fully-devoted follower of Christ means being indifferent to this world and all its encumbrances so that we can follow Him and share in all that He has for us in the future.

He who loses his life for the sake of Christ will find it.

LOSING YOU LIFE

When the rich young ruler came to Jesus, he was unwilling to sacrifice his riches to inherit treasure in the kingdom.[44] Jesus told the disciples that it is hard (not impossible) for a rich man to enter the kingdom of heaven/kingdom of God. Here, as elsewhere, the kingdom being discussed is the expected literal reign of Messiah.

The rich young ruler, knowing what it was like to rule in the present age, wanted to find out what the requirements were to rule in the age to come. When he found out, he went away grieving because he was hoping to have his cake and eat it too; he was hoping that he could rule during his lifetime and then rule again in the glorious kingdom that was coming. When he learned that he would have to make sacrifices during this lifetime on earth in order to qualify to rule in the age to come, he gave up the future for the abundance he enjoyed in the present.

This is an essential lesson in discipleship: *sacrifices are required.*

On account of the disciples' many personal sacrifices, in contrast to the rich young ruler who would not sacrifice his material resources, Jesus promised the disciples thrones when He return to earth to "sit on His glorious throne."[45] Sitting on thrones ruling over the twelve tribes of Israel is not the same thing as being saved and being part of the foundation of the church. Jesus' conditional promise to the twelve apostles is yet another indication of the earthly purpose of His incarnation and the literalness of His earthly reign as Messiah-King.

An essential lesson in discipleship: sacrifices are required.

Discipleship is a process which denotes "an orientation more than a state. It is a journey, and not an arrival."[46] The orientation is to a deeper commitment to Christ with a course that is focused upon the rewards in the coming kingdom of Christ. As the kingdom is the most important orientation of the Father, it goes hand-in-hand with the emphasis upon discipleship.

But remember, this must be done "by faith" as we intimately walk with Jesus. If not, we too run the risk of presenting only "wood, hay, [and] straw."[47] Being saved does not guarantee that everything we do is worthy or good; it must be done by faith in His life to empower you.

FAITHFULNESS IS KEY: BE CHOICE

Jesus gave the parable of the wedding feast[48] to illustrate that we must earn the kingdom. Here the kingdom is compared to "a king who gave a wedding feast for his son."[49] While all were invited to the feast, (i.e. the kingdom), some refuse the invitation and were disciplined for their refusal. This is a clear picture of the nation of Israel who, at the very time of Jesus' speaking the parable, were plotting against Him and planning His arrest and death.

After the refusal of the first invitation the invite is directed to all, whether good or evil.[50] And the guests come and fill the celebration. There is one man who responded to the invitation (he is saved) but did not clothe himself appropriately for the celebration. It is this man who is bound hand and foot and cast into the darkness outside, where there "will be weeping and gnashing of teeth."[51]

The summary statement by Jesus clarifies the intent of the parable: Many are called (literally, "invited"), but few are chosen.

The word *chosen* has confused many here, but can be resolved quite simply. The word translated "chosen" is actually an adjective, not a verb, and should be translated "choice" instead of chosen. As Gordon Olson writes, "It must be translated: 'Many are invited, but few are choice.'"[52] Thus being choice is a qualitative term indicating who is worthy by response to the invitation and self-preparation (in this case, appropriate clothing) through practical obedience.

Later, Jesus revealed to John that at the marriage supper of the Lamb,[53] those who make up the bride are clothed "in fine linen, bright and clean; for the fine linen is the righteous acts of the saints."[54] And just a few verses later we read, "The armies which are in heaven, clothed in fine linen, white and clean, were following Him on white horses."[55] I think the connection is obvious. The man in the parable responded to the invitation (he was saved) but had not clothed himself appropriately (in righteous acts).

This passage is not about heaven; it is about the kingdom. God does not "choose" some to be saved eternally and not others, for He is a heavenly Father who loves the whole world and desires all men to be saved.[56] What the parable is saying is that the kingdom has been offered to all but rejected by some, and that even those who are inclined to the invitation must make themselves choice in order to participate and possess.

We must be faithful.

We must be choice!

No regrets!

THE ROLE OF SUFFERING

Persevering to the end doesn't mean that we never experience pain or never fall down, but that we always get up. And often those things which cause us to fall are the pains and heartaches of this life which promise, in their ominous tones, to keep us down.

But as C. S. Lewis so aptly said, "God whispers to us in our pleasures, speaks in our conscience, but shouts in our pain: it is His megaphone to rouse a deaf world."[57]

Often times the difficulties and trials are essential elements to our training and preparation. Jesus taught His disciples that there is a direct connection between living for the kingdom and persecution,[58] suffering,[59] and the cost of discipleship.[60]

History has provided us a long list of faithful servants who have suffered greatly for the cause of Christ, many even to the point of death. As the second-century theologian Tertullian wrote, "The blood of martyrs is the seed of the church." And the list of just such people continues on even to this day. I am sure that rewards in the kingdom will be doled out in great number to them and all who suffer to any degree.

There is neither trial nor pain which we endure in faith that God will not reward in His kingdom.

Paul and others also taught the same.[61] By faith alone we become heirs of God, but an additional inheritance is ours as "fellow heirs with Christ"[62] which is gained through patiently enduring suffering like Christ.[63] This inheritance will be realized in the millennial kingdom, the place where our future glory is experienced.[64]

Paul spoke proudly of the church in Thessalonica on account of their "perseverance and faith in the midst of...persecutions and afflictions,"[65] which was a way they would be "considered worthy of the kingdom of God, for which indeed you are suffering."[66]

Suffering is not only tolerable, it is worth it in light of the future outcome. Paul, who suffered much, said, "I consider that the sufferings of this present time are not worthy to be compared with the glory that is to be revealed to us."[67]

This broken-down world has an expiration date. So remember that the "momentary, light affliction is producing for us an eternal weight of glory far beyond all comparison."[68]

St Ambrose said, "The Devil tempts that he might destroy; God tests that He might crown."

NOTES

1 Romans 7:18.
2 2 Corinthians 5:7.
3 James 4:8.
4 Romans 6:4.
5 Galatians 2:20.
6 Hebrews 11:6.
7 1 John 1:7.
8 John 15:4.
9 John 15:5.
10 Romans 14:23.
11 Hebrews 11:6.
12 Matthew 6:33.
13 See Romans 5:12–21.
14 Proverbs 22:6.
15 Proverbs 29:15.
16 1 Corinthians 3:1.
17 See Hebrews 5:11–14; Ephesians 4:14–15.
18 Matthew 28:19, emphasis mine.
19 Acts 1:8.
20 Acts 1:7.
21 2 Corinthians 5:19
22 Matthew 28:19–20.
23 Matthew 4:19; Mark 1:17.
24 Johnston M. Cheney and Stanley Ellisen, *The Story of the Greatest Life: A Unique Blending of the Four Gospels* (n.p.: Paradise Publishers, 1996), 58.
25 Jeremiah 16:14–16.
26 Matthew 9:37–38.
27 See Isaiah 17:11; Jeremiah 51:33; Hosea 6:11; Joel 3:13.
28 See Hosea 6:11.
29 Matthew 10:5–8.
30 Acts 1:8.
31 See Matthew 10:22–25.
32 See Matthew 10:22.
33 See Matthew 10:26–31.
34 Matthew 10:32.
35 See Matthew 25:21, 23; Luke 19:17.
36 Revelation 3:5
37 Matthew 10:33.
38 2 Timothy 2:12.
39 Matthew 10:37, 39.
40 Luke 14:26.
41 Charles C. Bing, "Coming to Terms with Discipleship," *Journal of the Grace Evangelical Society*, spring 1992, vol. 5:1.
42 Matthew 16:24–25, 27, emphasis mine.
43 See Matthew 13:39, 49; 25:31.
44 While the initial request by the young ruler is "What must I do to obtain

eternal life?" the context is clear that the life he is seeking is kingdom (cf. vv. 23–24, 27–30).

45 Matthew 19:28.

46 Bing, "Coming to Terms with Discipleship."

47 1 Corinthians 3:12.

48 See Matthew 22:1–14.

49 Matthew 22:2.

50 See Matthew 22:10.

51 Matthew 22:13.

52 C. Gordon Olson, *Getting the Gospel Right: A Balanced View of Salvation Truth* (Global Gospel Publishers, 2002), 278.

53 Revelation 19:7.

54 Revelation 19:8.

55 Revelation 19:14.

56 See John 3:16; 2 Timothy 2.

57 C. S. Lewis, *The Problem of Pain* (New York: HarperOne, 2001), 91.

58 See Matthew 5:10, 11; Luke 6:22; 22:28–29.

59 See Matthew 5:10–12.

60 See Matthew 10:34–39.

61 See Romans 8:18; 2 Corinthians 4:17; 1 Peter 4:12–19.

62 Romans 8:17.

63 Ibid.

64 See Romans 8:17b–30.

65 2 Thessalonians 1:4.

66 2 Thessalonians 1:5.

67 Romans 8:18.

68 2 Corinthians 4:17.

SEVENTEEN

LIVING MOTIVATED

Success is not final, failure is not fatal: it is the courage to continue that counts.

Winston Churchill

Here you are: at the end of the book. You were diligent and persevered; you made it! You finished well.

And here, at the end of this book, you hopefully find that you understand God's plan more completely. You have a bird's-eye view of all that He created and even the *why* for His creation. You now know, if you didn't before, that it's all about His glory; that all He made will culminate in the display of His majesty as His kingdom is accomplished on earth for all of creation to see; that the truth of the kingdom is proclaimed in Scripture from Genesis to Revelation, without compromise to God's promises or His nature.

You've learned the difference between heaven, eternity, and the kingdom, and you now understand absolutely that one's salvation is based upon grace alone, not on works. The fragile state of your salvation was a myth. Living in fear, shame, and guilt is totally unnecessary.

And you've seen that not all who are saved will be given the same quantity of reward in the kingdom. Our inheritance in the coming kingdom is a reward, the prize God gives to His children who have earned it in works they've done in faith, as they've dressed themselves in garments of righteousness. And you've seen that being a disciple of Christ is at the heart of who we are to be (by faith) and what we are to do (by faith).

We have already seen that there is no guarantee that it will always be easy. In fact, oftentimes it will be downright difficult. There will be days when you, like all others, will focus on the trial, not Jesus, and feel you have no gas in the tank.

You will feel weary. You may feel tired. Your strength may wane and your focus become blurred. How then, can you finish well?

How can you go on when this life is so hard?

God has given the motivation each of us needs to be disciples, faithful to the end.

Motivation is what drives actions. It is *motive in action*.

MOTIVATED OR MANIPULATED?

It has been apparent through and through that the teaching on the kingdom is intended to give us purpose and motivation to live toward this end. The kingdom must become our aim and that which we strive for. God's kingdom can and should be a primary motivation that fuels our faithful living for His glory now and for the age to come.

The kingdom is by no means the only motivation, but it is certainly one of prominence. At times God motivates us by reminding us how great and awesome He is, how great and awesome are His actions toward us in love, or how great and awesome are His benefits to those who walk in close intimacy with Him. It is not about my motivation or my favorite motivation, but the motivations He reveals and chooses to use in our lives.

We never know when God will choose to use any of the various ways to motivate us, but we must be aware of all so that we are prepared and receptive.

If we compare the way the church has attempted to motivate throughout the years with the way God actually does motivate, the contrast is striking. The church has tried to motivate people either by fear of losing their salvation or by casting doubts on whether a person was genuinely saved. Both methods are manipulative and use fear in connection with eternal salvation or our standing before God. Very harmful!

And if the method is not fear, then the other favorable option has been guilt.

I cannot begin to recall the vast number of people I have counseled or talked with over the years of ministry where the grind and burden of this inherently legalistic teaching had completely worn them down. Pages could be filled recounting all the testimonies of how this difference in thinking has radically changed lives for the glory of God. Here is one example of a lady who grew up in the church but struggled greatly with feeling adequate for God:

> Many Bible passages made me feel really uneasy about God and my security. My relationship with God was filled with angst. I knew He died for me, and I knew I didn't deserve it. Somehow, I got all the Scriptures about salvation, predestination, and rewards all mixed up.
>
> God seemed far away and judgmental. This was serious stuff, and I had to measure up. I would have times of just giving up and thinking that I wouldn't make it to heaven because it was just too hard.
>
> When you began preaching about the kingdom I was amazed, and soon many of my scriptural puzzle pieces were slipping into place.... It feels radical sometimes, but the Bible is starting to fit together, and I am not afraid anymore.
>
> *Becky M.*

If my many years of ministry have proven anything, her example of suffering under pain and guilt is not an anomaly among those who occupy the pews. Sadly!

But God does not motivate us with guilt and shame. By far the predominant motivation through the pages of Scripture is reward in the coming Messianic reign of Jesus Christ. God wants to motivate us by what lies ahead, and He uses that future reward to remind, encourage, challenge, and lovingly nudge us along to "grow in the grace and knowledge of our Lord and Savior"[1] and follow our Lord until His return, of which we know not the hour or the day.

FIND US FAITHFUL

Despite the reality of His impending rejection, Jesus taught the disciples that He would certainly return and His return could come at any time. His return was then, and is now, *imminent*. He told His disciples that He might return when they least expected it, so they were to be ready.[2] Thus we too are to be ready.

We need to live in light of the reality that our accountability for rewards may be tomorrow, or *TODAY*. We must live every day faithful with the stewardships He entrusts to us, that we may be found "so doing when He comes."[3]

This sense of urgency and faithfulness is the point being taught in the parable of the sensible servant,[4] the parable of the ten virgins,[5] and the parable of the talents.[6] The bottom line to all three of these parables is expressed in the first where we read: "Blessed is that slave whom his master finds so doing when he comes."[7] The reward for the faithful servant is great millennial reward. The consequence for the believer who is not persevering is loss of millennial reward.

> *Our accountability for rewards may be tomorrow, or today.*

Losing the prize will bring the Christian great remorse. This is seen in the fact that in the parable, the unfaithful servant is "cut... in pieces and [assigned] a place with the hypocrites; in that place there will be weeping and gnashing of teeth."[8] This is paralleled, in the parable of the ten virgins, by those who are not allowed to go in "with him to the wedding feast"[9] and again in the parable of the talents when the "wicked, lazy slave"[10] is cast "into the outer darkness; in that place there will be weeping and gnashing of teeth."[11]

Before you push the panic button, remember that these are parables, stories which are cast alongside a truth to teach a principle.

The "outer darkness" is a metaphor for being excluded from certain events or aspects of the kingdom, or a portion of the inheritance to rule as reward. Darkness outside is not hell. Charles Stanley comments about the darkness outside when he writes that it "represents not so much an actual place as it does a sphere of influence and privilege...it is not a geographical area."[12]

Loss of inheritance and privilege is the point. Those who are caught unaware and unfaithful at His return will suffer loss in relation to their rewards in the coming kingdom.

The weeping and gnashing of teeth is another metaphor that means there will be sadness and grief in light of the loss. Another comment from Stanley is helpful: "Just as those who are found faithful will rejoice, so those who suffer loss will weep. As some are celebrated for their faithfulness, others will gnash their teeth in frustration over their shortsightedness and greed."[13]

In his first epistle of John, we are told that living in abiding fellowship with Christ today creates confidence in the heart of the believer as he looks forward to standing in His presence at His second coming.[14] To not abide will result in "[shrinking] away from Him in shame at His coming."[15] This verse does not broach our eternal/positional acceptance before God when He comes; rather it describes the confidence we can have when He comes and finds us ready. Likewise, James also indicates that a reason for being patient and steadfast is on account of the nearness (imminence) of the Lord's return.[16]

What does living in light of His imminent return look like?

Let me illustrate what living with this perspective should look like.

To live with an understanding of His imminent return is like living with a pregnant wife in her final trimester. A husband is much more attentive. No matter where he goes he always has his cell phone on; he postpones out-of-town travel; and he checks in on her regularly because the baby could come any day. He might still do many everyday things (e.g., go to work, play golf, take in movie, play golf [yes, I said golf twice], etc.), but the expectancy changes the way he does those things and the significance he places on them. That is the idea of urgency in light of imminence.

Put it all together and what we learn is that the disciple of Jesus Christ should persevere in a walk of faithfulness, abide in fellowship, and live with urgency in light of His imminent return.

KINGDOM MOTIVATION IS RIGHT

The King and His kingdom ought to fuel our passion. Being motivated by reward is not selfish.

Read that again: *it is not selfish or wrong to live for rewards or seek His kingdom.*

The only warning Jesus ever gave the disciples in this regard was about "being competitive" about rewards. When asked by the disciples about who would be greatest in the kingdom, Jesus told them that "unless you are converted (lit., 'turned' [*strephō* in Greek]; see NASB margin reading) and become like children, you will not enter the kingdom of heaven."[17] At a minimum "not entering the kingdom" is an indication of being excluded from the greatness (which is what the disciples were seeking) of their inheritance. The condition for kingdom participation for the eternally saved disciples and all who follow is humility;[18] it is not about being greater than another fellow disciple but through humility realizing their own personal greatness in the kingdom to come. We are not in a competition with one another, and God does not grade on a curve.

While Jesus is correcting their competitive mind-set, He is not discrediting the proper place of motivation for rewards. C. S. Lewis once said:

If we consider the staggering nature of the rewards promised in the Gospels, it would seem that our Lord finds our desires, not too strong, but too weak. We are half-hearted creatures...like an ignorant child who wants to go on making mud pies in a slum because he cannot imagine what is meant by the offer of a holiday at the sea. We are far too easily pleased.[19]

And Erwin Lutzer touches on this very subject:

It is not selfish to want Christ's approval. He wants us to win the right to rule with Him in the kingdom, and that should be our passionate yearning.... Christ often and unapologetically motivated the disciples with the prospect of rewards.[20]

Understanding and appreciating the role of being properly motivated by rewards for the kingdom is essential to our spiritual growth and maturation. It is a motive which drives action. We need training to help us realize that our heavenly Father has a lot He is offering us, but at the same time He doesn't owe us anything. As disciples we must live by faith with urgency and perseverance, otherwise we may have serious regrets.

Time and opportunity are of the essence.

"RUN, FORREST, RUN!"

In the movie *Forrest Gump*, young Forrest is being chased by school bullies while Jenny yells, "Run, Forrest, run!" And run he did...so far, and so fast, that his leg braces broke off and fell to pieces. Running saved his life (so to speak)!

The author of the book of Hebrews tells us that we are all in a race and we must run: "Let us also lay aside every encumbrance and the sin which so easily entangles us, and let us run with endurance the race that is set before us, fixing our eyes on Jesus."[21]

The running of our own race is one that should be marked by endurance. Life is not a sprint, it is a marathon, so we need to be as light on our feet as we can and run in such a way that we may finish the course. Persevering, running with endurance, to the end is how we run to win. And the only way to do that is by "fixing our eyes on Jesus"—another illustration of faith.

We must run to the end. It was not until the end of Paul's life that he himself knew he had run his race so as to win because he "finished the course."[22] There should be no *give up* or *quit* in a disciple of Jesus Christ. How we finish, and the fact that we finish, are both important.

> *There should be no give up or quit in a disciple of Christ.*

Too many people are bound up by guilt of the past, or entangled with the encumbrances of the world, or held by sin that exerts a tight control and restricts their breathing. In order to finish the race we need to confess the sin,[23] get our eyes off the material world and off the past, and turn our eyes upon Jesus. Even if we fall flat on our faces (time and time again), we must get up and finish our race. If we fall and find ourselves lying and wallowing in our own self-pity, we must get up and finish the race.

For many years I have cherished a poem that illustrates this point well. The poem is entitled "The Race."[24] It's about a young boy who sets out to race against his peers with a cheering crowd of parents and friends looking on. The boy runs faster in his mind than with his legs, and he repeatedly falls. Each time he finds himself on the ground, he catches a glimpse of his father's face or hears his voice in the crowd; this inspires him to rise and run again. After the third attempt to run and yet another fall, he is totally defeated and ready to give up. The conclusion of the poem is as follows:

> Defeat! He lay there silently.
> A tear dropped from his eye.
> "There's no sense running anymore!
> Three strikes I'm out! Why try?
> I've lost, so what's the use?" he thought.
> "I'll live with my disgrace."
> But then he thought about his dad,
> Who soon he'd have to face.
> "Get up," an echo sounded low,
> "You haven't lost at all,
> For all you have to do to win
> Is rise each time you fall.
> Get up!" the echo urged him on,
> "Get up and take your place!
> You were not meant for failure here!
> Get up and win that race!"
> So, up he rose to run once more,
> Refusing to forfeit,
> And he resolved that win or lose,
> At least he wouldn't quit.

So far behind the others now,
The most he'd ever been,
Still he gave it all he had
And ran like he could win.

Three times he'd fallen stumbling,
Three times he rose again.
Too far behind to hope to win,
He still ran to the end.

They cheered another boy who crossed
The line and won first place,
Head high and proud and happy—
No falling, no disgrace.

But, when the fallen youngster
Crossed the line, in last place,
The crowd gave him a greater cheer
For finishing the race.

And even though he came in last
With head bowed low, un-proud,
You would have thought he'd won the race,
To listen to the crowd.

And to his dad he sadly said,
"I didn't do so well."
"To me, you won," his father said.
"You rose each time you fell."

And now when things seem dark and bleak
And difficult to face,
The memory of that little boy
Helps me in my own race.

For all of life is like that race,
With ups and downs and all.

And all I have to do to win
Is rise each time I fall.
    And when depression and despair
Shout loudly in my face,
Another voice within me says,

"Get up and win that race!"

The devil is screaming in our ear that we have lost, we've failed, it's too late; but we must resist the devil and get up and win our race. If we run so as to win and finish the course, there will be "laid up for [us] the crown of righteousness."[25]

Is it difficult at times to keep running the race? Unquestionably!

Some days it is even a challenge to get out of bed.

But if you are going to run…run that you may win!

Persevere and finish well.

NOTES

1 2 Peter 3:18.
2 See Matthew 24:44.
3 Matthew 24:46.
4 See Matthew 45–51.
5 See Matthew 25:1–13.
6 See Matthew 25:14–30.
7 Matthew 24:46.
8 Matthew 24:51.
9 Matthew 25:10.
10 Matthew 25:26.
11 Matthew 25:30.
12 Stanley, *Eternal Security: Can You Be Sure?* 127.
13 Ibid., 128.
14 See 1 John 2:28.
15 Ibid.
16 See James 5:8.
17 Matthew 18: 3.
18 See Matthew 18:4.
19 C. S. Lewis, *The Weight of Glory* (New York: HarperOne, 2001).
20 Lutzer, *Your Eternal Reward,* 16–17.
21 Hebrews 12:1–2.
22 2 Timothy 4:7.
23 1 John 1:9.
24 "The Race" is attributed to Dr. D. H. Groberg.
25 2 Timothy 4:8.

LAST WORDS

Come, Lord Jesus.

Revelation 22:20

The closing words of the Bible serve as a fitting close to this book as well. These words are in the book of Revelation and are the last recorded words of Jesus.

After describing in great detail the events of the end times, His second coming and earthly reign, and the eternal state, Jesus concludes by saying,

"Behold, I am coming quickly, and My reward is with Me, to render to every man according to what He has done.... Yes, I am coming quickly."[1]

And the apostle John's response: "Amen. Come, Lord Jesus."[2]

I cannot imagine a better way to conclude...*you can't improve on perfection*!

May it be our prayer as well: "Amen. Come, Lord Jesus."

NOTES

1 Revelation 22:12, 20.
2 Revelation 22:20.